INFORMATIVE SPEAKING

SCOTT, FORESMAN'S \/\/\/\/ COLLEGE SPEECH SERIES

THEODORE CLEVENGER, JR.
GENERAL EDITOR
FLORIDA STATE UNIVERSITY

THOMAS H. OLBRICHT
PENNSYLVANIA STATE UNIVERSITY

INFORMATIVE SPEAKING

DOUGLAS EHNINGER
CONSULTING EDITOR IN SPEECH
STATE UNIVERSITY OF IOWA

SCOTT, FORESMAN AND COMPANY

Library of Congress Catalog Card No. 68-16502
Copyright © 1968 by Scott, Foresman and Company, Glenview, Illinois 60025.
All Rights Reserved. Printed in the United States of America.

Regional offices of Scott, Foresman and Company are located in
Atlanta, Dallas, Glenview, Palo Alto, and Oakland, N.J.

FOREWORD

Variety is the keynote of undergraduate instruction in speech today. In some institutions of higher learning the basic speech course deals with public speaking; in others, with the fundamentals of speech; in still others, with an introduction to speech communication theory. Moreover, within these broad categories, as one moves from school to school and even from instructor to instructor within the same department, one finds that the basic speech course differs greatly in both activity and content. Subject matter that is taught in the introductory course at one institution is reserved for advanced courses at another.

One reason for this state of affairs is that the beginning undergraduate instruction in speech encompasses a wide range of subject matter – far more than can be offered in a single course. From this wealth of topics, instructors and course committees must select material that can be organized into a meaningful pattern of instruction. In addition, since the needs of students in various institutions and curricula differ considerably, textbooks that try to cover an entire semester's work have proved increasingly unable to bear the whole burden of undergraduate instruction. Writing a good survey text is further hindered by the rapid advances in knowledge and research taking place in the field. It is clear that more flexible instructional material is required.

In response to that need, Scott, Foresman's College Speech Series has been designed to provide maximum adaptibility to varying instructional goals. Our objective is to make it possible for the instructor to combine just those units of content which best serve the needs of his course: particular subject matter selected for a certain population of students at a given time. The format of the series has developed from that goal. Each title focuses on a single topic, which is developed by an "expert" in much fuller detail than is possible in a survey textbook. Each is independent of the others. The titles were chosen for minimal overlap, and no book in the series requires mastery of any other as a prerequisite for understanding. Of course, where appropriate, the authors have cross-referenced one another for purposes of fuller or more specialized treatment, so that the series, being integrated, offers a common philosophy. Each book is independent yet is also part of a consistent and comprehensive whole.

But the books of this series represent something more than a new format for instructional reading. Each provides an original analysis in depth, relying on recent theoretic advances and bringing to bear the most useful information available. The series is therefore something more than a subdivision and expansion of the typical survey textbook for the first course in speech; each book presents information and theoretical insights not heretofore available to the undergraduate student.

In some cases, it may prove desirable to build a beginning speech course around several topics selected from the series. In others, a single volume may be used to fill a void or to develop a particular topic in greater depth than does the survey textbook. Different sections of the same course may use the same general textbook but study from different volumes of this series in order to emphasize topics according to special needs. For many advanced or specialized courses, a particular book of this series may be used as the principal textbook, serving as the point of departure for extensive supplementary readings and special projects. Thus, this series may be used in a variety of ways at many different instructional levels, depending on the needs of the students, the goals of instruction, and the insight and imagination of the instructor.

Theodore Clevenger, Jr.
General Editor

CONTENTS

PREFACE

This book grew out of the conviction that something could be said about the characteristics of effective informative speaking. Informative speaking is required of a speaker when an audience demands clarification of a particular idea or subject. It thus differs from persuasion in its purpose. When a speaker is confronted by a persuasive task, he devotes his attention to change of audience attitude or action.

Informative Speaking early establishes the importance of an audience-centered approach to speaking, and the idea is expanded and substantiated throughout the book. An effort has been made to draw upon whatever insights into the informative act are available, regardless of the discipline in which the informing takes place. In drawing a perspective for organizing informative speeches, I have relied heavily upon the insights gained by work in programmed learning. The discussion of language has been set within the context of both contemporary philosophy and psychology of language. In some instances an indebtedness to information and learning theory will be recognized. But since principles from these disciplines are not always directly applicable to the construction of a rhetoric of informing, I have had to distill my insights on informing from observation of and experience with informative communication in a number of different contexts.

This book is designed for use in various educational enterprises. In particular, it should prove helpful for the informative-speaking unit of courses in general speech and public speaking. In addition, it should find use as a textbook for a basic informative-speaking course and for courses on a higher level concerned primarily with the rhetoric of informing. An effort has been made to employ examples which reflect the future informative tasks of students as they enter such professions as engineering, architecture, medicine, and teaching.

I am indebted to a number of people for their help at various stages of this project. I am pleased to express appreciation to my colleagues Henry W. Johnstone, Jr., and Richard B. Gregg of The Pennsylvania State University, who read an early draft of the manuscript and made many helpful suggestions. But I am especially indebted to Theodore Clevenger, Jr., of the Florida State University for his invaluable editorial efforts. I also wish to thank Mrs. Carol Embury of Scott, Foresman for her detailed attention to the manuscript. Perhaps, too, I should mention Dorothy, Suzanne, Eloise, Joel, and Adele, who though not having much to do with the actual writing of the book, have nevertheless through the years provided many occasions for informing, and thus have made a contribution which is not immediately obvious.

Thomas H. Olbricht

I.

THE EMERGENCE OF

INFORMATIVE COMMUNICATION

Our civilization stands at the threshold of enormous informative tasks. Modern developments have multiplied information and complicated informative materials. Yet we have made a commitment that everyone has the right to know, and this right demands vehicles of communication which effectively convey complexities without distortion. Specialization is the order of the day, and most informative communication is, directly or indirectly, between the specialist and the layman. The informative speaker must be concerned with more than having a specialist's accurate information. If he is to successfully communicate that information, he must pay attention to the manner in which complex ideas can best be explained to audiences of varying levels of competence.

To make the task of the informative communicator clear, attention must be given to the unique nature of informative communication. In this chapter we will explore the characteristics of such discourse by examining the historical emergence of this form of communication.

COMMUNICATION IN THE ANCIENT WORLD

The terms *information* and *informing* appear frequently in today's vocabulary, but these words have not always been used so widely. Why is it that only modern man has written about the rhetoric of informing? Perhaps in seeking a historical answer to this question we will come to better understand the role which informative communication plays in contemporary civilization.

In the ancient world those who wrote about discourse designated their discipline *rhetoric*. These men were concerned about persuasive speaking, but gave little attention to informing. For Aristotle, rhetoric was "the faculty of discovering the possible means of persuasion in reference to any subject whatever."[1] Both Cicero and Quintilian wrote at length on rhetoric and noted that in the rhetorical works which preceded them, informing received little attention.[2] Quintilian took pains to note that informative communication has a distinct nature, but he failed to tell us much about it. One introductory section of the prepared speech the ancients labeled the *narratio*, which, because of our English word *narration,* might appear to mean "informative." But Quintilian and others advised the speaker to marshal the *narratio* so as to achieve the greatest possible persuasive force.[3]

When we examine the rhetorical works of the ancient world it becomes clear that the authors of the day did not attempt to produce a definitive work on *informing* in the same way that they wrote treatises on *persuasion.* The one possible exception is Augustine, who in a short work titled *De Catechizandis Rudibus* discusses the distinctive features of informing when the priest is teaching the catechism. George Campbell, an eighteenth-century British churchman, is accredited with being the first rhetorician to give special attention to informative communication, but even he was chiefly interested in "enlightening the understanding" as a means of obtaining a "persuasive effect."[4]

I. A. Richards, in his *Philosophy of Rhetoric*, states that "neutral exposition is a very special limited use of language, comparatively a late development. . . ."[5] In considering language, Richards draws the same conclusion as we did in examining the rhetoricians. But his claim goes further by indicating that the ancients were little concerned with informative discourse because little informative communication was to be found in the ancient world. What case can be made for Richards' claim?

One would expect that the appropriate place to locate informing would be in teaching situations; but, strangely enough, even teaching in Greece and Rome was looked upon as an argumentative affair.

1. Aristotle, *Rhetorica*, I, 2, 1.
2. Cicero, *De Oratore*, II, 64; Quintilian, *Institutio Oratoria*, IV, iii, 12.
3. *Institutio Oratoria*, III, ii, 31. Cf. George Kennedy, *The Art of Persuasion in Greece* (Princeton, N.J.: Princeton University Press, 1963), p. 11.
4. George Campbell, *The Philosophy of Rhetoric*, ed. Lloyd F. Bitzer (Carbondale, Ill.: Southern Illinois University Press, 1963). Cf. Edwin Black *Rhetorical Criticism* (New York: The Macmillam Company), pp. 11–16.
5. I. A. Richards, *The Philosophy of Rhetoric* (New York: Oxford University Press, 1936), p. 40.

Plato, in his dialogues, attempted to teach his views by argument rather than by informing, since education for him was defined as bringing forth what is already in the mind rather than pouring facts into a sponge-like mind, in the manner of educational philosophy since John Locke. Plato's predecessor, Protagoras, taught that it is possible to argue against any position. The result was a method of teaching by *antilogy*, or debate, an approach which left its mark on Greek philosophy, science, and culture.[6] Much ancient teaching was, as Karl Popper noted, in the "tradition of critical discussion."[7] Even Aristotle, who thought that man learned much from observing the world, nevertheless conveyed his knowledge largely by argument. He seems to have shared the predisposition of the Greeks that most knowledge is arguable.

One can follow argumentative or persuasive discourse into the Roman world, for Cicero and Augustine frequently wrote in dialogues, and even those who did not (for example, Lucretius and Quintilian) produced documents that were essentially argumentative, both in their approach and in the attitudes they evoked.

As strange as it may seem to us, even medicine was learned through argument. H. I. Marrou tells us that during the time of the Roman Empire, the physicians in the Museum in Ephesus formed an association and had a yearly medical debate over such matters as methods in surgery and the instruments to be used.[8] It is significant that the Greeks never collected volumes of conclusions either in medicine or science, nor did they prepare abstracts. Whenever scientific conclusions were presented, they also included the arguments by which the conclusions were derived. Scientific instruction was therefore basically argumentative, even though certain teachers might claim that their arguments were beyond dispute. Before information — in the sense we are using it here — could emerge, it was necessary to adopt a radically different attitude toward the material to be communicated.

Another reason why informing was not really known to the ancients is that a different situation existed in regard to the dissemination of specialized knowledge. Until modern times, instruction in the various skills and professions was more by imitation than verbal communication, and specialized knowledge was zealously guarded to keep it in the family or guild. In the modern world, by contrast, most instruction is verbal, and we are committed to making

6. H. I. Marrou, *A History of Education in Antiquity,* trans. George Lamb (New York: Sheed & Ward, 1956), p. 51.
7. Karl Popper, *Conjectures and Refutations* (New York: Basic Books, Inc., Publishers, 1962), pp. 148ff.
8. Marrou, p. 193.

knowledge available to anyone who wishes to obtain it. By examining the manner in which dissemination of specialized knowledge has changed, we can better understand the nature of informative communication.

The educational centers of the ancient world did little teaching of the skills or trades. Such training was the province of the family or, later, of the guilds. Excluded from ancient education were disciplines which have vital roles in contemporary educational institutions, such as ceramics, mining, engineering, and commerce. One learned the skills of these occupations via apprenticeship, much of which involved observing, and then doing, rather than verbal instruction. R. Freeman Butts writes:

> One of the most important cultural agencies of education, however, was not touched by the schools, and that was the preparation for engaging in an occupation or trade. Vocational education was a matter with which the schools of Athens did not concern themselves. It was left to a more or less informal system of apprenticeship. In this respect Athenian education continued along primitive tribal lines. Training for a vocation was cared for in family groups as the father taught his son his own occupational tasks. Apprenticeship also became somewhat specialized and formalized as children were taken into shops and households where they were taught the elements of a trade.[9]

Since the teaching of the trades was private rather than public, it is easy to see why those who wrote about public communication, e.g., Aristotle and Cicero, did not discuss informative communication of this sort.

Medicine also was taught largely by observation. H. L. Marrou notes, "The study of medicine in Graeco-Roman times still meant getting in with a practicing physician and doing one's apprenticeship under him."[10] The apprenticeship may have included reading the classics on medicine—for example, Hippocrates—but because no one system of medicine prevailed, these writings were largely argumentative in nature. What is especially significant is that training in the medical profession continued largely through private apprenticeship even until well into the nineteenth century. The first medical school established in North America was at the University of Penn-

9. R. Freeman Butts, *A Cultural History of Western Education* (New York: McGraw-Hill Book Company, 1955), pp. 43–44.
10. H. I. Marrou, *A History of Education in Antiquity*, trans. George Lamb (New York: Sheed & Ward, 1956), p. 193.

sylvania in 1765. It probably is not a mere coincidence that along with the establishment of such schools went a growing awareness of informative discourse.

A similar situation prevailed in the training for most trades and professions until the latter part of the nineteenth century. It has only been in the past one hundred years that many occupations, previously learned by apprenticeship, have grown so complex as to warrant their own divisions in university curricula or special institutes and training programs in industry. As the complexity of these skills and professions increases, those who enter must learn more and more background knowledge. The result is an increasing role for informative discourse in the contemporary world.

Not only did much training take place without verbal communication in early times, but that training which emerged was guarded jealously by those who obtained it. Today we are committed to the proposition that everyone who desires to know has the right to do so. (The only exceptions pertain to national defense and industrial secrets.) Such a commitment on any widespread scale, however, is very recent. In the classical period specialized knowledge was preserved by families; in medieval times trade guilds maintained secrecy; and even more recently, before patent laws were adequately enforced, inventors went to great lengths to guard the secrecy surrounding their creations.

The history of glassmaking illustrates these various efforts to maintain secrecy. The making of glass emerged as an art in Egypt in the Second Millennium B.C. Manufacturing was limited to certain families, and outsiders were prevented from learning the techniques involved. Later, medieval Venice became known for its excellent glass wares. Knowledge of the various Venetian processes were preserved in family groups, but in spite of family secrecy, the city fathers became concerned lest the secrets spread abroad. So they passed laws forbidding the glassworkers from leaving the city or teaching their secrets to outsiders. Dire penalties were executed against both offending glassmakers and their families. In the sixteenth century, glassmaking emerged at L'Altare, near Genoa, where, in contrast to Venice, the workers taught their knowledge to those from other cities, but this relative freedom was the exception rather than the rule.[11]

In medicine, even into the nineteenth century, the same conditions prevailed. Doctors developed their own systems and perfected their own medications. Neither the techniques nor the formulae for the medications were available to the general public. If a young man wished to practice medicine he apprenticed himself to an older

11. W. B. Honey, *Glass: A Handbook and a Guide* (London: Victoria and Albert Museum, 1946).

doctor, whose methods he then learned. When the young doctor went out on his own, he was required for a period of time to give the older doctor a percentage of his earnings.

A good case, therefore, emerges for the conclusion that the availability of information is a unique feature of our modern world. In our time anyone who wishes to know how different types of glass are made has little difficulty finding the information in books, encyclopedias, and essays. The same is true of medical knowledge. One who wishes to learn about new medical techniques or pharmaceuticals need only turn to popular feature and news magazines or even newspapers. If he wishes information of a more technical sort, it is readily available in medical journals. Only physicians may legally *practice* medicine, but anyone can *learn* about it.

From this discussion we can supply at least a partial answer to our question concerning why only modern man has written about the rhetoric of informing. Ancient man, unlike his modern counterpart, employed the term "informing" infrequently because he did not conceive his knowledge as information, he employed little verbal communication in training for the trades, and he jealously protected whatever technical knowledge he happened upon. These considerations shed a ray of light on the nature of informative discourse. Whenever knowledge is conceived as disputable both by the speaker and the auditor, it is difficult for communication to proceed as information. In order for informing to emerge as a mode of communication, a subject matter must attain the privileged status of being beyond dispute, at least for some sizable group of people. Also, instruction must become verbal and specialized knowledge readily available if informative discourse is to emerge. The existence of these three conditions today has placed a premium on the speaker or writer who is able to convey complex ideas in such a manner that the uninformed can digest the information.

COMMUNICATION IN THE MODERN WORLD

In spite of the fact that informative speaking was unknown in the ancient world, the roots of modern developments in communication *are* located in the past. We noted that Augustine may have been the first to give serious attention to informative discourse. Perhaps the reason was that Augustine wished to convey knowledge that many in his time considered beyond dispute. In the first three centuries of the Christian era the Christians *argued* their way into Roman culture – as can be seen by the number of apologies that remain. But by the fourth century many people in the empire had come to look upon Christianity as having an *indisputable* message concerning the situation of man in the world. Because of these new developments the main task of the churchman was not so much to *argue a case,* but to *set forth the teaching* of the church. Augustine saw this as the situation when someone presented himself to the church to be catechized. In the book written to help the priest in the task of catechizing, he pointed out that the catechumen who comes to the priest "has already made up his mind to be a Christian."[12] This person would not be inclined to argue with the priest, for he would already look upon the message of the church as beyond dispute. As the Middle Ages advanced, more and more men accepted the teaching of the church as factual—that is, as comprising information rather than argument.

The emergence of modern science

But such confidence in the teaching of the church did not last. The decline of the medieval church marked the beginning of a new era, and once again controversy broke out in Western civilization. Modern science began to make some advances, but had not yet reached the stage where scientific conclusions could be presented as information. In fact, Francis Bacon contended that few, if any, of the scientific conclusions of his time were beyond dispute. He proposed that all contemporary scientific knowledge be subjected to investigation and be rejected if it did not stand. Science, in Bacon's view, was to be conveyed not as information beyond dispute but as tentative statements to be subjected to argument.

> For the sciences have hitherto been delivered as if both the teacher and the learner desired to receive errors by consent—the teacher pursuing that method which procures the greatest belief to his doctrine, not that which most commodiously submits it to examination, whilst the learner desires present satisfaction without waiting for a just inquiry as if more concerned not to doubt than not to mistake.[13]

It is not clear whether Bacon envisioned scientific propositions which could be presented as information, in the manner of twentieth-century science. It is obvious, however, that for his own day Bacon thought that science had to argue its way stage by stage. Therefore, the type of communication with which he was most concerned was persuasion.[14]

In the generation after Bacon, René Descartes (1596-1650)

12. Augustine, *De Catechizandis Rudibus,* 12.
13. Francis Bacon, *Advancement of Learning,* VI, 2.
14. See Karl R. Wallace, *Francis Bacon on Communication and Rhetoric* (Chapel Hill: University of North Carolina Press, 1943).

pointed science in a new direction. He agreed with Bacon that much current scientific knowledge had to be overthrown. He was distressed that under the prevailing scientific methods "nothing solid can have been built on foundations so unstable."[15] He thereupon proceeded to lay more solid foundations by the geometrization of all studies of the physical world. In this manner he hoped to reach scientific conclusions that were beyond dispute and that could be communicated as information rather than controversial material. However, scientific development did not follow Descartes' mathematical model, but instead turned to the empirical groundwork of Hume, Mill, and Comte. Later scientists did take Descartes' advice, however, in searching for propositions which can be firmly established beyond dispute. When technicians came to accept the possibility of indisputable scientific conclusions, a whole new world for informative discourse arose. When a body of scientific conclusions accumulated, conclusions which men were no longer inclined to dispute, then scientific communication had to do with the reporting of facts—hence the emergence of informative communication.

Logical positivism

In the nineteenth century, science was largely looked upon as a body of indisputable conclusions. Logical positivism in the twentieth century helped further this attitude, and wherever such an outlook prevails among scientists today communication is affected.[16] A number of scientists and philosophers of science today, however, dispute the positivistic view. These include such men as Karl Popper, J. Bronowski, and A. C. Ewing,[17] who argue that it is difficult to exclude the human element in framing scientific propositions, and hence science is always colored by human thought and culture. Scientific propositions are therefore always open to further modification. Popper, in particular, attacks the "accumulation" theory of science in which new conclusions are continually added to propositions already established. For him, science is a discipline that proceeds by controversy. In the positivist view, on the other hand, informative discourse is fundamental to science, especially in introducing the novice into the discipline, even as the catechism is fundamental in introducing one to the church.

15. René Descartes, *Discours de la methode*, I.
16. See for example, Ernest G. Bormann, *Theory and Research in the Communicative Arts* (New York: Holt, Rinehart & Winston, Inc., 1965), pp. 33–119.
17. Karl Popper, *Conjectures and Refutations* (New York: Basic Books, Inc., Publishers, 1963). J. Bronowski, *The Common Sense of Science* (New York: Vintage Books, n.d.). A. C. Ewing, *The Fundamental Questions of Philosophy* (New York: P. F. Collier, Inc., 1962), pp. 31–58.

The manner in which informing as communication shifted from the medieval church to contemporary science is pointed up in a decisive way by the experience of William G. Pollard, who is both a physicist and an Episcopalian clergyman.

It is true that when I give a popular lecture as a physicist, I can count on having an audience which is completely sold in advance on the validity, importance, and undeniable truth of the enterprise of physics as a whole. . . . It is equally true that whenever I give a popular lecture on a theological topic, I can count on having an audience equally convinced in advance that religion, although possibly proper, respectable, and even admirable, is nevertheless a private peculiarity of individual people and therefore essentially unreal and invalid. . . . But it has often struck me that, had God given it to me to live in the sixth century or even the twelfth instead of the twentieth, the situation would have been exactly reversed. Then when I spoke on Christianity my audience would have been convinced in advance of the complete validity and universal truth of what I represented.[18]

Pollard makes it clear that what a given culture in a given period of history considers as information may not be information in another culture at another time.

Audience receptiveness

History shows that whenever some view becomes accepted by a large segment of a people, argument or persuasion about that subject diminishes and informing emerges. When these conditions prevail, persons concerned with communication take up the study of informing. Augustine was one of the first, and his comments were expanded in the Middle Ages by such men as Rabanus Maurus in *De Institutione Clericorum* (819 A.D.). In modern times, attention to informative communication began with George Campbell and Joseph Priestley, who set up categories of "enlightening the understanding" and "exposition" in their rhetorics.[19] With the rise of modern rhetoric almost every book on writing and speaking contains a chapter on informing, narration, or exposition.

It would therefore appear that information is what any sizable group of people accepts as information. However, the fact that a group accepts something as information does not mean that that infor-

18. William G. Pollard, *Commemorative Papers from Iowa State College Centennial* (Ames: Iowa State University Press, 1958), pp. 49–69.
19. George Campbell, *The Philosophy of Rhetoric*, 1776. Joseph Priestley, *Lectures on Oratory and Criticism*, 1777.

mation is necessarily true. Different cultures accept divergent materials as information because they have a different view of truth. From the standpoint of the rhetoric of information, material can be conveyed as information whenever the audience accepts it as such, regardless of whether it is true according to some universal standard. If an audience will not accept information as true, then the speaker cannot *inform*, but must *argue* in an effort to get the audience to accept it as true. If a speaker takes advantage of a receptive audience by informing them of something he knows is not true, he is a charlatan.

The question of what is true is not an easy one and obviously cannot be discussed sufficiently in this book. But it is too simple to say that informative communication is "the conveying of what is factual." We have already set forth the problem of cultural and universal factuality. The scientist is usually looked to in our time as the person with the most "universal" factual knowledge, but even in science, in spite of claims to the contrary, a human element remains. So J. Bronowski writes:

> For science is not the blank record of facts, but the search for order within the facts. And the truth of science is not truth to fact, which can never be more than approximate, but the truth of the laws which we see within the facts. And this kind of truth is as difficult and as human as the sense of truth in a painting which is not a photograph or the feeling of emotional truth in a movement in music.[20]

It would therefore appear that "fact" is not the best term to describe scientific truth, nor the best word to describe the content of informative discourse. We are concerned in this book not only with the facts of informative communication, but also with what the facts mean – a difference which we shall see has important implications for a rhetoric of informing. Computers may adequately convey facts, but in human communication the human elements come to the surface.

INFORMATIVE COMMUNICATION IN THE CONTEMPORARY WORLD

Finally, our insight into informative communication will be enhanced if we can find some applications in the contemporary world. Inform-

---

20. J. Bronowski, *The Common Sense of Science* (New York: Vintage Books, n.d.), p. 129. Cf. Karl Popper, *Conjectures and Refutations* (New York: Basic Books, Inc., Publishers, 1963); and *Philosophical Writings of Peirce*, ed. Justus Buchler (New York: Dover Publications, Inc., 1955), p. 249.

ative tasks in our world are numerous, but we shall take time here to examine only a few.

Because of automation, many new approaches and skills are required in industry and much effort is being expended to train employees in these new operations. An indication of industry's growing demand for those who can supply specialized information is the newly created company which has no product other than technical information. One such business is the Sunderland Company of Peoria, Illinois, which has as its sole purpose advising industries in the use of computers. Representatives of the corporation inform company executives of the manner in which computers may be employed most advantageously in their business. Thus we can see how the complexity of modern industry has created an informative situation, where businessmen are willing to listen to specialists whenever knowledge is available. The executives do not wish to argue and do not need to be persuaded. They invite to their office the man who knows, to be "catechized" in much the same manner as the men who came to the priests of the church in the days of Augustine.

Not only have "informative" companies emerged, but industry is employing all sorts of professional men as consultants. The industrial audience seeking the advice of the specialist is far greater than in any previous historical epoch. Training programs also are multiplying within industry. Some of these are persuasive in nature inasmuch as employees are encouraged to adopt certain procedural approaches. But increasingly the programs' sole purpose is to convey to employees new and complex developments. Such programs assume that the employee is open to the new information, and hence a situation is created for informative discourse. Colleges and universities have, in addition to their regular curricula, created many programs for industry, along with continuing or adult education. Programs of this sort are created for professional men—for example, tax institutes for lawyers and accountants, medical colloquiums for doctors, and conferences for executives and ministers.

A primary setting for informing is, of course, the educational institution. Argument and persuasion are present in teaching, especially in good teaching; but in a number of disciplines, controversy is absent from the beginning course, since the student has not yet attained the degree of sophistication essential for arguing with the teacher. The assumption in physics, for example, is that a student must master the basic theorems before he can argue the assumptions underlying contemporary physical theories. His initial problem is to understand the models through which the physicist attempts to explain the universe. The task of the teacher is clarification in this case, and not argument. While the increasing magnitude of knowledge poses a serious challenge to communication, the increasing complexity of that knowledge perhaps presents an even more pressing one. Frank G. Favorite refers to these developments by pointing out that each of the various biological disciplines has its own vocabulary, jargon, methodologies, and models.[21] Various attempts at popularization are made through the news magazines and such journals as *Scientific American.* Speakers also are invited by industry and service clubs to disseminate information of this sort. But it is not only the layman who has difficulty in understanding the specialist. In the chemistry department at Cornell University a tacit understanding prevails that only one professor on a doctoral candidate's committee is expected to understand fully the research submitted. When specialization has reached this level we are faced with a tremendous communication problem, not only from the standpoint of the sheer volume of information, but also from the standpoint of the ability to comprehend it. Seldom in the past have educated men been so unable to communicate with each other, as C. P. Snow so ably depicts in his book, *The Two Cultures and the Scientific Revolution.*[22] In our commitment to the right of everyone to know, we must also be committed to devise means of making such communication possible.

Of course, communication technique is not the panacea for the situation which specialization has thrust upon us. Mere knowledge of better means of communication will not by itself make the complex understandable in our complicated world. Some concepts are of such magnitude—for example, the theory of relativity—that not only are effective vehicles of communication required, but also a background in numerous disciplines such as physics, mathematics, chemistry, and, perhaps, philosophy. Communication technique cannot overcome the absence of conceptual perspective. Conversely, however, it is possible to communicate information so badly that even the man who knows the subject matter has difficulty understanding what is said. The way in which information is conveyed, though not sufficient in itself to elicit understanding in every case, clearly has something to do with whether material is understood.

The task of the one concerned with informative discourse is to find the most effective means of communicating materials of varying complexities to differing audiences. It is to this task of developing *communication insight* that this book is dedicated.

21. Frank G. Favorite, "Interim Solutions to the Bioscience Communications Problem," *Bioscience,* February 1964, p. 18.
22. C. P. Snow, *The Two Cultures and the Scientific Revolution* (New York: Cambridge University Press, 1962).

Projects

1. Prepare a report on two classes in which you are enrolled, one of which deals in subject matter that is received by the students as "informative," and one of which deals in subject matter that is received by the students as "persuasive." Cite one or more critical incidents which, according to your observations, characterize the difference between the two courses.
2. Try to imagine making an informative speech and a persuasive speech, both on the same topic. What differences in the audience would lead you to adopt these different modes of address? Would your own attitude and purpose differ from one speech to the other? Would the content of your speech differ? Could the same speech be considered persuasive by one auditor and informative by another member of the same audience? If so, would one auditor be right and the other wrong?
3. Prepare a speech on the manner in which knowledge in the profession you expect to enter became public knowledge. That is, when did the profession first permit public dissemination of its knowledge? If you are not sure what you plan to do, speak on some profession that interests you.
4. Prepare a speech on the situations in which informing takes place in the profession you expect to enter, and discuss some of the problems of informing in that field.
5. For class discussion, be prepared to talk about the amount of communicative material, both spoken and written, connected with your future profession. Do the complexities of ideas in the profession pose any special problems?

2.

AN AUDIENCE-CENTERED

APPROACH TO

INFORMATIVE DISCOURSE

In examining the emergence of informative discourse in Western civilization and its role in contemporary culture, we have acquired an insight into the nature of informing as distinguished from persuading. In order to set forth the characteristics of informing in a more systematic way, let us now examine several different grounds for this distinction.

Before proceeding, however, we need to realize that a rigid distinction between informative and persuasive discourse is impossible, even if one considers only short segments of communications rather than whole discourses. The most realistic approach is a continuum with gradations running from informing to persuading. These gradations might be described and defined in such a way as to give us an increased understanding of these various degrees of discourse. Arranged along a continuum, they would look something like this:

INFORMING ┼┼┼┼┼┼┼┼┼┼┼┼┼┼┼┼ PERSUADING

But unless one is prepared to write a rhetoric for each of the gradations, such a continuum makes little contribution to the rhetoric of informing. In this book we are concerned chiefly with discourse that lies at the extreme left of the continuum. In other words, we shall be describing what the sociologist Max Weber designates an "ideal type."[1] We will first consider the nature of informative discourse as

___

1. See *From Max Weber: Essays in Sociology,* trans. and ed. Hans H. Gerth and C. Wright Mills (New York: Oxford University Press, 1946).

it would occur in an ideal form. Once we understand the ideal type, we can introduce modifications which will help us to understand the less pure forms.

TRADITIONAL MEANS OF DISTINGUISHING INFORMING FROM PERSUADING

Scholars have designated various beginning points in distinguishing between informing and persuading. One traditional manner of delineating types of discourse is to contrast the *purposes* of the communication. It is said that whereas the purpose of informing is to secure understanding, the purpose of persuading is to secure a change of commitment.[2] One difficulty with this distinction is that what the speaker intends as informing may result in change of belief, and what he intends as persuasion often enhances the understanding.

Another manner of making the contrast is to say that informing (reporting) is limited to facts and expert opinions and interpretations, while persuasion has to do with stimulation and emotion.[3] With this distinction, however, arises the difficulty that speeches designated as informative produce an emotional affect on some auditors in some situations, while persuasive speeches frequently contain material which is considered factual.

Faced with these difficulties, the tendency in recent years has been to question the distinction between informing and persuading, and to consider all communication as persuasion. David K. Berlo, for example, argues that "all use of language has a persuasive dimension, that one cannot communicate at all without some attempt to persuade, in one way or another."[4]

We must concede that a definitive distinction between persuasion and informing is difficult. Nevertheless, it is helpful to the speaker and writer to know some rhetorical differences between the speech in which a physicist is asked to explain quantum mechanics to a Lions Club, and one in which he desires contributions from the club in order to bring Negroes from the South to be educated in a northern high school. One difference is bound to be a variance in audience attitude. It is unlikely in the first situation that anyone in the audience would wish to argue with the physicist, and therefore his task is one of clarification. (An audience of physicists, on the other hand, might

2. George Campbell, *The Philosophy of Rhetoric,* ed. Lloyd F. Bitzer (Carbondale, Ill.: Southern Illinois University Press, 1963). Cf. Donald C. Bryant and Karl R. Wallace, *Fundamentals of Public Speaking* (New York: Appleton-Century-Crofts, 1960), p. 97.
3. James H. McBurney and Ernest J. Wrage, *The Art of Good Speech* (New York: Prentice-Hall, Inc., 1953), pp. 268, 322.
4. David K. Berlo, *The Process of Communication* (New York: Holt, Rinehart & Winston, Inc., 1960), p. 9.

argue with the speaker.) With the second subject, however, many members would feel as qualified to judge the merits of the proposal as the physicist. He would therefore be presumptuous if he set out merely to inform about the effort: rather, he would need to argue that bringing in the Negroes is the proper course of action. In this case, his discourse would of necessity be argumentative or persuasive in nature.

By delineating speech types in terms of audience attitudes, one can usually determine whether the task of the speaker is to clarify or to persuade. As we shall see in Chapters Three through Seven of this book, clarification requires rhetorical techniques which differ from persuasion. Moreover, with an audience-centered differentiation, any question of whether the informative discourse is *emotive* or *factual* according to some universal criterion is no longer consequential. The distinguishing criterion will be whether the discourse is emotive or factual to a specific audience.

METHODS OF CLASSIFYING SPEECHES

In order to clarify what is involved in an audience-centered approach to distinguishing speech types, we need to examine four approaches to classifying speeches. These are (1) situation-centered, (2) speaker-centered, (3) message-centered, and (4) audience-centered.

The situation-centered approach

The oldest ground for classifying speeches, the one used by Aristotle, was essentially situation-centered. This is not to say that Aristotle was unconcerned with the purpose of the discourse or the subject matter, or that his rhetoric itself was situation-centered. But in classifying speeches his approach was to search out the different situations in which speeches were given and to label his discourse accordingly. His classifications included the assembly (deliberative), the court (forensic), and *agora* or theatre (epideictic) speeches.[5] Aristotle refers to three kinds of hearers in these circumstances, but he fails to discuss at any length how auditors in any one of the three situations differ from those in the other two, especially in terms of any commitments they might have. Aristotle did not discuss informative speeches, but if we were to add the informative category to his other three, the situation in which it would be found would probably be the classroom.

5. Aristotle, *The Rhetorica*, I, 3.

The difficulty with classifying speeches by the situations in which they are given is that communication does not consistently unfold according to type in the situation. For example, in the assembly, which supposedly is deliberative in speech type, decisions are often based on legal rulings, with the result that forensic speaking emerges. This happened in many famous speeches.[6] The same problem arises if one attempts to treat all discourse in the teaching situation as if it were informative. In many disciplines (such as philosophy) teaching proceeds as much by argument and persuasion as it does by informing. One thereby concludes that though the situation-centered approach may provide a loose classification, another distinction is required if we are to describe types of speeches with precision.

The speaker-centered approach

Historians of rhetoric point out that George Campbell made a significant contribution to rhetorical theory when he departed from the older manner of classifying speeches according to situations and distinguished them in terms of the intentions of the speaker. According to Campbell's analysis, the possible intentions of the speaker are "to enlighten the understanding, to please the imagination, to move the passions, or to influence the will."[7] Most twentieth-century authors of speech textbooks have followed Campbell in this speaker-centered approach.[8] It appears, in these books, that it is the speaker who determines whether the speech is to be informative or persuasive, and that the commitments of the audience can be ignored. At any rate, one finds no discussion of the difference between the audience to whom it is possible to speak informatively, and the one whom the communication must move persuasively.

It is important that a speaker take these differences into consideration. An effort to inform when the audience rejects the message as informative is futile. A student in one of my speech classes before the 1964 presidential election decided to give an informative speech on Senator Goldwater. She thought she was objective about the Senator, but those classmates who were opposed to the Senator thought her speech persuasive: only those who favored the Senator regarded the speech as informative. The student intended to give an informative speech, but the audience, because of its attitudes toward Senator Goldwater, considered the speech persuasive, and poor persuasion at that. In this case the options were either to give a

6. George Kennedy, *The Art of Persuasion in Greece* (Princeton, N.J.: Princeton University Press, 1963), p. 261.
7. George Campbell, *The Philosophy of Rhetoric*, pp. 23–24.
8. See, for example, Donald C. Bryant and Karl R. Wallace, *Fundamentals of Public Speaking* (New York: Appleton-Century-Crofts), p. 97.

persuasive speech about the Senator, or else to speak on another subject. Likewise, it is possible that a speaker may intend to persuade, only to have his arguments received as information. An example might be a renowned biologist who argues against the merits of polyunsaturated fats only to have the audience accept what he says as information. Because of the biologist's fame, the listeners accept his statements without further examination. It may be that for some audiences and on some topics a speaker has an option of either persuading or informing, but it is the audience who by their attitudes makes that option possible, not the speaker by his intention.

The speaker-intent differentiation is, like all definitions, arbitrary. All the rhetorician wishes to declare by such a definition is that by "informing" *he means* a communication in which informing is intended by the speaker, and by "persuading" *he means* a communication in which the speaker intends to persuade. Such a definition is no more arbitrary than any other, but it is not as helpful as an audience-centered differentiation, since the audience is the final judge as to the type of communication it will accept and the effectiveness of a speech is dependent on the speaker's correct analysis of the audience's willingness to accept information. Perhaps the most logical position for one who wishes to focus on speaker intent is the one Berlo takes: namely, that all communication is persuasive.

The message-centered approach

The message-centered approach to speech classification is primarily employed by those, such as speech critics and philosophers, who examine messages, and not by those concerned with speakers and audiences. The critic or philosopher, for example, classifies discourse *after* it has been presented. He is concerned with whether the message appears to be either arguing a case or appealing for action; if so, he concludes it is persuasive. If the message consists primarily of what he considers factual material, he treats it as informative discourse. Those who work with information theory likewise approach communication from the standpoint of the message,[9] as do those involved in language analysis[10] and general semantics.[11] In information theory (for example, as it is applied to designing electronic communication systems) the focus is on the message and specifically on techniques which will systematically increase the amount of information that can be transmitted through the system

9. Colin Cherry, *On Human Communication* (Cambridge, Mass.: The Technology Press, M.I.T., 1957).
10. I. A. Richards, *The Philosophy of Rhetoric* (New York: Oxford University Press, 1936).
11. Alfred Korzybski, *Science and Sanity* (Lancaster, Pa.: Science Press, 1941).

per unit of time. Little attention was given to the audience in early formulations of the theory, since the assumption was that all audiences would receive the message alike. Recently, modifications have been attempted in order to account for different audiences. Language analysts also focus on the message, for their interest is in language with universal rather than individual meanings. These philosophers admit, of course, that individuals and audiences employ the same words in different ways, but they set out specifically to overcome such individual uses of language; thus, their project might be described as *therapeutic*. The general semanticist likewise advances a therapeutic program by trying to make language meanings more universal. Furthermore, Alfred Korzybski, the father of general semantics, opposed truth that is truth only for the individual. From this point of view, audience differences cannot be the ground for communication theory, since if they exist, they need to be overcome.[12] Because of the language analyst and the general semanticist's therapeutic approach to language, their study of communication is message-centered. But if we take the position that individual differences in audiences are to be accepted, then we need a communication theory that can adjust to these differences.[13]

An audience-centered approach

Obviously, something may be learned from a message-centered approach, but it ignores an element present in every communicative act – the person of the audience.

Upon reading or hearing a message, a critic may determine to his own satisfaction whether it is argumentative and emotive, or clarifying and objective. But not infrequently what is objective to the critic may prove emotive to a given audience. The explanation of the manner in which public debt differs from personal debt may not arouse emotional involvement in the critic, but it might in an audience convinced that government debt involves the same dangers as personal debt. A speaker giving a speech on civil rights to a Hudson Bay audience might receive little emotional response, but the same speech delivered in Jackson, Mississippi, might arouse considerable emotion. These differences in audience reactions exist and must be taken into account. It is surprising that in spite of the fact that rhetoricians through the centuries have talked about audience-centered rhetoric, very little attention has been given to an audience-centered ground for classifying speeches. A few theorists

12. *Ibid.*, pp. xliii ff.
13. See the final chapter for further discussion, and also my article, "The Self as a Philosophical Ground of Rhetoric," *The Pennsylvania Speech Annual*, September 1964, pp. 28–36.

have noted that the audience must be considered in making this distinction, but the point has not been explored systematically. Gilman, Aly, and Reid note that informative discourse demands a certain disposition on the part of the audience.

> Informing proceeds only when the audience is receptive. A speaker who talks today about the circulation of the blood assumes that the principle is accepted. Since no prejudices exist, he proceeds with complete freedom to report the result of scientific inquiry. Before Harvey discovered that the blood circulates, however, the same speech would have been highly controversial.[14]

Hovland, Janis, and Kelley also recognize that the communicative approach, whether informative or persuasive, depends on the audience.

> Typically the classroom audience has initial expectations that the communicator's conclusions will be the "correct answers." Hence, *acceptance* can usually be taken for granted and the primary problems are those of maintaining attention and insuring comprehension. In the case of persuasive communications, however, motivation to accept or reject becomes a major consideration, and may sometimes even influence the degree of attention and comprehension.[15]

The audience predisposition, they go on to say, determines the type of discourse possible.

> When formal instruction is given, the audience ordinarily is set to learn, and voluntarily accepts the status of students in relation to an instructor. This is generally not the case with persuasive communications in everyday life.[16]

In spite of these observations, an audience-centered differentiation of speeches has never been widely adopted. Part of the reason may be that communication theorists have not taken into account a wide enough range of audiences. We need a method for classifying speeches which will consider varying audience attitudes, not only for American audiences, but for audiences throughout the world,

---

14. Wilbur E. Gilman, Bower Aly, and Loren D. Reid, *The Fundamentals of Speaking* (New York: The Macmillan Company, 1951), p. 290.
15. Carl I. Hovland, Irving L. Janis, and Harold H. Kelley, *Communication and Persuasion* (New Haven, Conn.: Yale University Press, 1953), p. 290.
16. *Ibid.*, p. 16.

and in all historical periods. To construct such a method, we must consider closely the relationship of the audience to the communication.

Many of the reasons why it is helpful to approach types of discourse from an audience-centered standpoint have already been set forth. We can summarize these reasons as follows:

(1) In the final analysis, the decision as to whether a message is argument or clarification, objective or emotional, is determined by the audience rather than by the speaker, the speech content, or the situation in which the speech is made.

(2) If a communicator first raises the question of whether his audience will accept his message as informative or persuasive, he is in a better position to select speech content and approach. If he fails to ascertain the task which the audience demands, his communication may well prove abortive.

(3) A speech critic can better judge a discourse when he determines its possible effects on a given audience. The critic offers a precarious judgment if he concludes that a discourse is informative without considering that it may not have appeared that way to the audience to whom it was delivered.

We now need to account for the forces which determine the receptiveness of an audience to an informative-type message. An audience will likely be open to an informative communication when (1) it considers the subject noncontroversial, or (2) if the subject is controversial, it has no strong commitments regarding it, and (3) it accepts the speaker as knowledgeable on the subject and without ulterior motives. If these conditions prevail, it is possible for a speaker to present an informative discourse. If not, a communication intended as informative will probably fail. We will discuss these requirements in greater detail in Chapter Three.

If an audience has a strong view on some topic, it will not appreciate a discourse which purports to be objective and undermines the intensity of the audience's commitment. A group of supporters of the Vietnam policy will not be impressed with an informative analysis of current developments if the analysis seems to be tending in the direction of withdrawal. Contrariwise, an audience that is emotionally involved on some subject seeks discourse which comes out strongly for the point of view which it holds. An audience that is adamant on the dangers of saturated fats or chemical pest and disease control will be more excited about a speech which supports their own point of view than one which does not. An informative speech on the subject may be tolerated, but those strongly opposed will tend to grow restive.

If a speaker is connected with a cause or is suspected of having an ulterior motive for speaking on the topic presented, he will have difficulty gaining acceptance of his material as information. A man known to be opposed to the United Nations will find it difficult to give an informative speech on that body, especially to an audience with a number of people who support it. A representative of a sales organization—for example, an auto salesman—will have difficulty getting a prospective buyer to believe that his talk about an automobile is purely informative. In either case, the communication which is most likely to secure the desired results would be persuasive.

In order for an audience to consider a speech informative, that speech must also be viewed as noncontroversial. It would be difficult to give an informative speech to most American audiences on flying saucers or unidentified flying objects. A speech on spiritualism which pretended to be informative, and which the speaker himself believed, would likely be suspect in America, though less so in Great Britain. The same would be true for a speech on extrasensory perception. Either speech would be more effective as a persuasive speech than as an informative one.

Informative communication is, then, best defined in terms of audience predisposition. Such a definition is capable of universal application inasmuch as no criteria are set forth to declare what the audience *ought* to consider as objective. In other words, the differentiation is relative to the audience. One need not be a relativist, however, to define informing in this manner; one needs only to agree that the audience ultimately determines the nature of a communication. A speaker might believe that what he is saying is true and feel that he needs merely to inform the audience; but it would be futile for him to do so if his audience did not accept his message as information. He would have to concede the need to persuade that particular audience, even though he felt the case for his "truth" was so strong that it did not need to be argued.

As suggested earlier in this chapter, we are describing an "ideal type" of informative discourse. In applying the definition to actual speaking situations, certain difficulties will arise. An auditor might be predisposed to accept a communication as informative until a certain point in the speech strikes him as controversial. In fact, such change of receptivity happens frequently. When it does, the speaker's most effective strategy, if he hopes to reach the listener, is to meet the objection and then move on. If, however, the speaker feels that the objections of that particular auditor are not crucial, or that he does not have time to discuss them adequately, he may decide to ignore the objections and continue speaking without stopping to argue. Speakers are always faced with this type of decision. The speaker who seeks to persuade must decide whom in the audience he hopes most to reach, in case the audience represents a wide range of opinions.

It is true that from an audience-centered standpoint very few segments of communication are altogether informative or persuasive. But this need not disturb our identification of an ideal type. Whenever conditions are open to clarification in any communication, according to our definition, that part of the communication falls under the rubric of informing. If in another unit of the same speech the communicator turns to persuasion, then that part of the communication must be considered persuasive.

We have, then, located informative discourse in situations in which an audience is predisposed to accept without argument what the speaker has to say. In the remainder of this book we will see how an audience-centered definition of informative discourse influences what we have to say about a rhetoric of information.

Projects

1. Select a controversial subject and attempt to give an informative speech on it. Before you speak, circulate an audience-attitude ballot. After the speech is completed, use the same ballot to see if any views have been changed. Also, on the second sheet ask each listener to indicate whether the speech was informative or persuasive. From these answers determine if what is intended as informing changes opinion. Also, determine if audience views correlate in any significant way with their judgment about the type of speech they have heard.
2. Select three or four speeches from some collection—for example, Arnold, Ehninger, and Gerber, *The Speaker's Resource Book* (Glenview, Ill.: Scott, Foresman and Company, 1966)—and write a short statement indicating whether they are informative or persuasive. Use each of the four methods of classifying speeches suggested in this chapter and see if your conclusion as to type differs according to the method you use.
3. Listen to a professor giving a lecture and determine whether he is informing or persuading. Decide which type of speech you think he is trying to use and which type the other students think he is using. Is it possible that the professor thinks he is arguing whereas the students consider it informing? Do students respond better to a teacher who clarifies rather than argues?
4. Voice disagreement with something said by a teacher or speaker who is giving an informative speech and see if he turns to persuasion.

3.

AUDIENCE ANALYSIS

FOR INFORMATIVE DISCOURSE

AUDIENCE, OCCASION, AND PREDICTION

The nature of the audience

For rhetorical analysis, an audience can consist of a bundle of universal characteristics, or it can consist of individuals with varying styles of living and understanding. If one thinks of the audience as having universal characteristics, he would claim with Bazarov in *Fathers and Children:* "People are like trees in a forest; no botanist would think of studying each individual birch tree."[1] Such a view of the audience would lead one to look for general audience traits, and many rhetoricians have recommended that speakers analyze their audiences in this manner.

If a speaker is going to generalize in this way about his audience, the proper starting point in preparing an informative speech is to determine how much most of the listeners probably know about the subject. To discover this the speaker will need to know some of the characteristics of tenth-graders, college graduates, steelworkers, or Puerto Ricans. He will then assume that he can generalize and know the background of any audience.

If, however, people are not as alike as trees, a different sort of analysis is required. The knowledge of tenth-graders on any subject matter is likely to vary greatly. For example, they will all have some knowledge of space probes, but some will choose to pursue knowledge

---

1. Ivan Turgenev, *Fathers and Children*, trans. Ernest J. Simmons (New York: Holt, Rinehart & Winston, Inc., 1963), p. 95.

about the space program and will be more sophisticated about it.[2] Information about what the *average* tenth-grader knows about space is of some value, but it will not be adequate for the astute analyzer of audiences. Universal traits are helpful in analyzing audiences, but they must constantly be refined to recognize group divergencies, and they become less useful when dealing with individuals. An audience analysis which treats audiences as being composed of individuals must give detailed attention to means of ascertaining individual differences in audiences: in this way this type of analysis differs from one which treats the audience as a bundle of universal traits.

Historical audience analysis

Historically, rhetoricians have approached audience analysis as if audiences consisted of universal traits. Aristotle, for example, argued that deliberation is significant as a human activity only if choice is possible.[3] He argued that there is a crucial difference between man and animals, based on man's facility for reasoning. But for Aristotle, all men who employed correct reasoning should end up thinking alike, depending, of course, on their age and level of development. Since reason provided a means of universality in mental life, all men at a given level should understand each other without difficulty; since they had the same body of knowledge from which to draw, they should all reach the same conclusions. This characteristic of Aristotle's philosophy is what philosophers call *nativism*. As his psychology and ethics were based on human types, so also was his audience analysis, inasmuch as he was searching for universal traits of human types.[4] Rhetorics based on eighteenth-century psychology were even less inclined than Aristotle to consider human differences. They saw even the emotions as universal human traits, and gave little attention to how emotions might differ from man to man. Modern statements on audience analysis follow the eighteenth-century tradition, since much psychology in America has been constructed along these lines. Perhaps there is a new trend based on individual-centered psychologies, but the movement is too current to have produced a very profound effect on our views of speech audiences.[5]

2. A detailed argument for human freedom is not possible here. See *Determinism and Freedom*, ed. Sidney Hook (New York: Collier Books, 1961).
3. Aristotle, *The Ethics*, Book III.
4. See J. A. K. Thomson's introduction to Aristotle's *Ethics* (Baltimore: Penguin Books, Inc.), pp. 23, 24.
5. Three examples are Gordon W. Allport, *Becoming* (New Haven, Conn.: Yale University Press, 1955); A. H. Maslow, *Motivation and Personality* (New York: Harper & Row, Publishers, 1954); and William Stephenson, *The Study of Behavior* (Chicago: University of Chicago Press, 1953). Raymond S. Ross, *Speech Communication* (Englewood Cliffs, N.J.: Prentice-Hall, Inc., 1965) gives attention to Maslow's motivation theory, but not in such a way as to systematically inform his communication theory.

The point of view which we shall adopt toward audience analysis therefore represents, to some degree, a departure from tradition. We shall look, not for universal similarities among auditors, but for the factors which predispose them to respond differently.

THE OCCASION FOR INFORMATIVE DISCOURSE

The amount of audience information a speaker must seek will depend on how well he already knows his audience. If he has had considerable personal contact with them he can predict knowledge and attitudes with little effort. If, however, he knows little about the audience, he must employ whatever sources of information about them are available.

In Chapter Two we discussed the three criteria which the speaker should consider if he hopes to inform. We will now consider in detail these three questions.

(1) *Does the audience look upon the subject as noncontroversial?* A student in a class presented what he intended as an informative speech during the controversy over polyunsaturated fats. In his speech he stated as fact that saturated fats increase the incidence of heart disease. After the speech a number of students argued with him; one or two of the challengers cited studies in which investigators had concluded differently. As a result, his total communication was put into question, some thinking that he had misinformation, and others that he was purposefully attempting to persuade in the guise of informing. Perhaps the student could not have predicted the audience reaction, but at least he should have known that opposing views existed, thereby giving the topic a controversial status. In states in which legalized gambling is under consideration, the subject is usually so controversial that it is difficult to present information, for the audience is likely to interpret any "information" as biased and arguable.

(2) *If the subject is controversial, how deeply is the audience committed on the topic?* In a state in which an attempt is being made to pass a right-to-work law, it is doubtful that a labor union would appreciate an informative speech about these laws. They might interpret the speaker's failure to oppose such laws as a sign that he supported the attempted legislation. Some independent unions, however, favor right-to-work laws if written in certain ways, and they might welcome an informative speech. In a similar manner, a fraternity faced with probation would have little interest in a discourse on the history of fraternity probation. Of more interest to them would be a persuasive speech indicating how they should behave in order to

avoid probation, or one indicating what the brotherhood should do in the event that it is placed on probation.

Conversely, if in the midst of a heated campaign for a right-to-work bill a speaker addresses an audience which favors the bill, while his audience senses that he himself opposes it, and he attempts to present both sides of the question as if he were uncommitted, it is doubtful that many in the audience will view his communication as information. The same reaction would likely result if a fraternity representative appeared before the board which threatened probation and attempted to pass off his communication as purely objective, uncolored by the desires of the fraternity. Of course, the board will want real information, but it will object to persuasion in the guise of information. The point is that the board will doubtless be skeptical of the ability of a person so emotionally involved to communicate real information.

If the commitments of a group are not strong one way or the other, even though a local or national controversy is raging, a speaker may employ either informative or persuasive speech.

(3) *Does the audience accept the speaker as authoritative, forthright, and without ulterior motives?* Unless he is a figure who commands national respect, it is likely that a speaker's image as an authority will vary from audience to audience. He should therefore be concerned with the manner in which particular audiences will receive him. If an audience links a communicator to a definite point of view and thinks he has something to gain by speaking on this topic, they will not accept the speech as informative, but view whatever the speaker may say as persuasion in the guise of information. A man who is head of a United Fund drive in a city will not receive as favorable a reaction if he attempts to give an informative speech about the United Fund, as if he honestly tries to persuade. Some of his audience would accuse him of juggling the facts in his "information." They would expect him to marshal his facts so as to secure the greatest results for the fund drive. Similarly, a fraternity member cannot expect to give an informative speech on fraternities during rush period to a group of students who dislike fraternities. They will expect persuasion from him and respond more favorably to it.

Now that we have seen how audience predispositions determine whether a speaker can present an informative discourse, we need to discover how one can determine audience predispositions. The speaker who has first-hand acquaintance with an audience needs only to consider how the audience will respond to him and the topic. His predictions about the audience should be much more accurate than one who does not know his listeners personally. This is why the man who adapts best to an audience often is not the one who is a communication expert, but the one who has a deep acquaintance with the people to whom he is to speak. As Aristotle stated, "It is in fact experience rather than theory that normally gets results."[6]

If, however, one is not acquainted with the audience, he must depend on means other than experience to obtain the needed information. The most likely source to ask is someone who knows the audience, particularly someone who has himself spoken to that audience. A community leader who has been asked to give speeches usually will be able to provide the best picture of the people in the community. But if it is not possible or desirable for the speaker to solicit information from someone on the scene, he must predict audience attitudes from what is known generally about people who live in a certain place and who belong to certain types of organizations, although, as we discussed earlier in this chapter, it is best to avoid these generalizations whenever possible. In order to assure some accuracy of prediction the speaker will need to know the age, occupation, nationality, religion, and other pertinent items about the audience.[7] Even if one has secured these data, however, the possibility is always present that the speaker might predict wrongly. A speech teacher once was invited to speak to a Future Farmers of America meeting at which he knew adults would be present, but expected fathers only. His prediction seemed safe; but as it turned out, mothers and sisters were also there. He found himself in a predicament because some of the humor he had planned was now out of place.

AUDIENCE KNOWLEDGE

Once a communicator ascertains that it is possible to convey information, he must determine how much the audience knows about the subject. (If the discourse were to be persuasive, in contrast, the speaker would need to know the audience's commitments on the topic and their needs in relation to the topic.) If a speaker is acquainted with an audience he will have a fairly accurate idea of what they know. This is especially true if he is himself a leader in the group.[8] If he is not, he needs a systematic method for predicting audience knowledge as accurately as possible. Often, by knowing some basic facts — such as age, level of education, and geographical area — one can predict the amount of audience knowledge with some accuracy.

6. Aristotle, *The Ethics*, VI, 7.
7. For a fuller treatment of this topic, see Paul D. Holtzman, *The Psychology of Speakers' Audiences*, in this series.
8. Research in social perception has established the ability of group members, especially leaders, to perceive the knowledge and views of those with whom they associate. See William W. Lambert and Wallace E. Lambert, *Social Psychology* (Englewood Cliffs, N.J.: Prentice-Hall, Inc., 1964), pp. 28ff., and J. E. Hochberg, *Perception* (Englewood Cliffs, N.J.: Prentice-Hall, Inc., 1964).

Before looking in a detailed manner at means of predicting what the audience knows on the subject, we need to ask what sort of information we need for purposes of adaptation. Specifically, the informative speaker needs to ascertain (1) the level at which he must commence, (2) the kinds of concepts known by the audience and upon which he can build, (3) how rapidly the audience is capable of grasping the content, and (4) the types of particular knowledge and interests they have, so that he can decide what types of analogies and examples may be the most helpful.

Factor analysis

The first step in a systematic program of predicting audience knowledge is factor analysis.[9]

Some factors that may be of help in estimating audience knowledge are: (1) age, (2) sex, (3) economic status, (4) occupation, (5) parent's occupation, (6) education, (7) intelligence, (8) group affiliations, (9) region of the country, (10) nationality, (11) community, (12) race, and (13) hobbies. It would be impossible, in discussing factor analysis, to say everything that can be said on every subject and audience. In order to give some indication of what is involved, four different types of situations and audiences will be discussed. Perhaps through such an examination of specific cases the method of individualistic audience analysis will become clear. Such detailed analyses are an *ideal,* however, and are probably more elaborate than is always possible. The four speech occasions which we will explore are: (1) a student who desires to inform a college class about Sigmund Freud's theory of dream interpretation, (2) a plant pathologist who has been invited to speak to a Grange in another state concerning control of plant diseases, (3) a teacher of literature who is to speak to a woman's club on "stream of consciousness" as a literary technique, and (4) a computer expert who has the task of explaining the use of a new computer to the executives of a chemical corporation in another region of the country.

EXAMPLE 1: "FREUD'S THEORY OF DREAM INTERPRETATION."
        Audience: College Class

Since the speaker's audience will be fellow students of approximately the same age, his task of factor analysis is somewhat simpli-

9. The term "factor analysis" is employed here as by political scientists. The factors are the items in the political situation such as geography, form of government, economics, etc. In psychology the same term has to do with a statistical method to account for the intercorrelations among test scores, a usage of the term which is clearly different from that employed here.

fied. He qualifies to give the talk because in selecting it he probably has read and studied in psychology more intensively than his auditors and therefore knows more about the topic than they do. (In this sense he is a "specialist.") If he is a student in a small college or in a speech class consisting of students from the same university college, he no doubt will know what sort of background his audience has in the topic. But in a large college in which students come from various divisions, the speaker probably won't even know what other courses the students are taking, much less how much background they have in his topic. The analysis here will suppose such a situation.

The student has three basic ways of finding out what the audience knows on his subject. (1) He can ask the instructor for data about the composition of the class, such as their majors and classification. (2) The data not available from the instructor can be collected from fellow students by personal interview. (3) He can consult the college catalog, which will tell him the specific courses required for students from different curricula, and at what level they are likely to take them.

Factors such as race and sex will be simple enough to observe, while others such as age, economic status, and nationality may possibly be acquired through observation. If the class has been in session for some time the student will have acquired some knowledge of his classmates' interests, hobbies, intelligence, and regional background by listening to them speak; he might even keep a record of interests revealed in speeches of the other students.

EXAMPLE 2: "CONTROL OF PLANT DISEASES."
Audience: Grange Meeting

The audience of the plant pathologist will consist chiefly of farmers, but factor analysis will still provide helpful information. The best method for obtaining data about the audience is to write the person extending the invitation, asking about the crops raised in the region, the types of diseases prevalent, and the climatic conditions. (Eleanor Roosevelt always insisted, before accepting an invitation to speak, that someone from the local scene supply her with data about the audience.) From the local informant the pathologist may, in addition, request information about the ages of the farmers, their educational level, and how well they keep up with current developments in disease control. Knowing the race or nationality of the farmers could, in some cases, be desirable data. In order to supplement the information supplied through correspondence, the pathologist could refer to reference works. From these he would find out the predominant crop of the region, the amount of rainfall and mean temperatures, and perhaps even information about disease control problems. If he has a friend who is a plant pathologist in the state he might write him requesting information not otherwise available.

EXAMPLE 3: "THE STREAM OF CONSCIOUSNESS."
Audience: Women's Club

In this case, the speaker will probably know something about her audience, since they are a local group. The main source of information will be the person extending the invitation or someone in the group whose analytical ability the speaker respects. She should try to obtain such information as the ages of the women, their education, major in college, economic level, and level of general intelligence. The friend may also know something about books the members are likely to have read or the study groups in which they have been involved.

EXAMPLE 4: "THE NEW COMPUTER."
Audience: Chemical Company Executives

The computer expert will first need to find out what previous experience the chemical corporation executives have had with computers. If computers have previously been sold to this company, he may be able to obtain this information from his own company records or request information from someone in the company. If this is not possible, he may seek a briefing upon arrival from either a secretary or one of the executives involved. The speaker will be interested in discovering the extent to which the executives have worked with computers, their ages, level of education, and area of specialization.

In these four specific speech occasions, we can see certain characteristics of factor analysis: in the first place, not all the factors are significant for every speech occasion. For example, nationality is not crucial for determining how much one knows about Freud; sex and economic status are not of much help in determining what farmers know about disease control; and group affiliations and hobbies are likely to be of little help in predicting what people know about computers. Even when all factors are applicable, some provide more information for certain communication occasions than for others. The factors most crucial for the student speaking on Freud are student major and classification; for the plant pathologist, the type of farming done; and for the literature professor, the amount and type of reading. Factors therefore need to be employed with discretion in order to secure the type of data most pertinent.

Prediction based on factor analysis data

When one has secured data about the audience via factor analysis, he has grounds for predicting the audience's level of knowledge. It should be borne in mind, however, that factor analysis by itself provides no information as to what the audience knows. The speaker rather is dependent upon the amount of information he is able to obtain about an audience with a given set of biographical data as determined by factor analysis.

EXAMPLE 1 (CONTINUED): "FREUD'S THEORY OF DREAM INTERPRETATION."

After the student has collected his data about an audience, he can use this data to predict the audience's actual knowledge of a subject. If he finds that three of the students are psychology majors, he will wish to discover the extent to which they have studied Freud. He might predict this by looking at the psychology books used, or by analyzing what he remembers from his own courses. He could also ask one of these students what he knows about Freud. He can discover what non-psychology majors should know by consulting the college catalog to see what psychology courses they are required to take, and at what stage they are required to take them.

In the preparation of this speech, the factor of specific previous education is the most significant, but other factors may provide additional insight. Economic status may be of some consequence inasmuch as students from the higher economic levels are at present more likely to have had relatives who have been under psychiatric care, or may themselves have been. Statistics on economic status and psychiatric care are available in books on mental health. The occupation of the parents may provide additional, though limited, information. If students have fathers who are psychologists or psychiatrists, they would probably have some knowledge on the subject. Since Freud's views are fairly complex, the predicted intelligence of the class will have some bearing. If some in the class cannot easily cope with complex ideas, the points must be explained with considerable care. Students from urban areas are more likely to know about Freud than students from rural communities.

With experience, the speaker can do this sort of stock-taking in rapid order. After scrutinizing the audience he should be in a good position to predict the point at which he can commence his speaking — a point which is neither too difficult nor too simple for his audience. Various levels of knowledge will be present among the students, and this may present a serious problem: The speaker must use discretion if he is to adapt to those from many different backgrounds.

EXAMPLE 2 (CONTINUED): "CONTROL OF PLANT DISEASES."

Correspondence, reference works, common knowledge, or other means will tell the speaker what crops are raised in the area his audience farms. With this Information he will be able to discover what types of diseases he should discuss. In addition, he will need to ascertain the amount of knowledge the farmers have on plant diseases and fungicides. He may draw upon his experience with other farmers or the experience of his colleagues. By knowing something about the ages and education of the farmers, he will have further indication of their knowledge. In prime farming areas younger farmers are likely to have studied recent fungicide developments in high school and some may have gone to agricultural school. (The plant pathologist can predict the level of education with some accuracy by finding out about the agricultural schools in the state – their number of graduates, their proximity to the community in which he is to speak, and the geographical distribution of their students.) If the region is noted for its successful farming, fungicide dealers are likely to have disseminated a great deal of information. In areas where the farm income is low, however, the information possessed by the audience is likely to be more elementary. Farm income in various areas can be readily discovered by looking in Department of Agriculture publications. Fungicide companies may also make available statistics concerning the type of fungicides sold in various regions of the country. The plant pathologist should also seek to find out what information, if any, the Grange provides its members about plant diseases and control. It will also help to know the type of farm journal popular in the region, how many farmers subscribe to it, and what recent material it has published on plant disease control.

Other factors may provide limited information. Group affiliations such as the American Farm Bureau or the Farmer's Union may provide some information. From these organizations one can discover what information they distribute and where their members are located. Some groups, such as Mennonite and Amish farmers, tend to employ primitive modes of agriculture, and would probably have little recent technical information. Sharecroppers would also be less likely to have up-to-date information.

An important difference between writing and speaking may be noted here. If the pathologist were writing a pamphlet for general distribution, he would project an image of the average farmer and adapt to it. But in a specific audience situation, if he wishes to adapt to the audience as much as possible, it is necessary to carefully predict what this particular audience knows on the subject. In communicating to a specific audience he can speak on their level and thus be more helpful than he could hope to be in a pamphlet written for general consumption. Much of the material in a pamphlet might not be relevant to a given group of farmers because of the type of farming in which they are engaged. The advantage of oral discourse is that it enables better audience adaptation. A speaker should capitalize on this advantage by finding out as much as possible about the audience.

EXAMPLE 3 (CONTINUED): "THE STREAM OF CONSCIOUSNESS"

The literature professor will need to ascertain whether any women in the club have read novels employing the stream-of-consciousness technique, such as James Joyce's *A Portrait of the Artist as a Young Man* or William Faulkner's *Sound and the Fury.* She will also need to know whether they have read any interpretative analyses of modern literature that may have discussed stream of consciousness. Finally, an estimation of the club's knowledge of psychology would be useful.

The factor most helpful in this case is the one concerning education. If most women are college-educated, the teacher can assume that they have read at least one novel employing the stream-of-consciousness form. By knowing the women's ages and the type of college from which they graduated, one would have a still better idea of the books they had read. One should also ask how many of the women are English or psychology majors. These women would probably have a good background in the subject.

Perhaps just as important as college training would be the type of reading the women have done in post-college years. Economic status and husband's occupation probably are the most highly predictive factors in this determination. Sociological studies report the average amounts of reading at the various economic levels; people in middle and, particularly, upper-middle classes tend to read more than those at other economic levels. Group affiliations, especially book club memberships, are also valid indicators of reading habits. Book clubs often solicit members from subscribers to such magazines as *Harper's* and *Saturday Review.* Studies show that the people who take these publications are mostly upper-middle class and above; therefore, they are probably better read than average. In addition to making this general observation, the speaker could find out what books the clubs have distributed in the past few years; this would give her specific information about her audience's reading. Finally, the speaker's own familiarity with the community should give her some idea of the type of reading done by the women.

EXAMPLE 4 (CONTINUED): "THE NEW COMPUTER"

Let us assume, for our analysis, that the chemical corporation already employs computers, but now wishes to purchase a new model. In this case, the auditors probably already have considerable background information. Inasmuch as the executives have worked with computers, the speaker may assume that they have already acquired a knowledge of the fundamentals of computer theory. The task of the company representative is to determine what the men know about computers from the other computers the corporation has used and then to build on the concepts already possessed. This requires a different rhetoric than if the audience were completely uninformed, as it might be in the case of the student explaining Freud to his classmates.

When a speaker is conveying information to a knowledgeable audience, factor analysis has limited usefulness. In this case, knowing about previous computers of the corporation is the most crucial information. Something is to be gained, however, from knowing the educational background and intelligence of the executives. If they have a background in mathematics, electronics, engineering, and physics, they will more fully appreciate the new information and will absorb it with minimal explanation. Since the plant produces chemicals, some general background along these lines can be expected. The speaker, in requesting information, could ask if any of the audience had college majors in these areas. The age of the executives might also reveal something about their level of knowledge; if they are middle-aged or older, their background knowledge in electronic data processing is likely to be inadequate, although one cannot depend fully on such a conclusion since good executives continue to master new concepts.

In speaking to an audience that is generally informed on a subject, the speaker usually has a good insight without extensive analysis as to the knowledge of the audience. Specialists frequently read papers at conventions or write for technical or scholarly journals. Of course, they have to keep their audience in mind, but it is not so much a matter of "prediction," since being in the profession assures first-hand knowledge of the audience. It is when the specialist speaks or writes for a group of specialists in a field other than his own that prediction of audience knowledge becomes crucial. Though they are more sophisticated than a general audience, they should be considered as one for the purpose of factor analysis. However, since the audience is probably more homogeneous than most, the best approach would be to ask someone in the group what his colleagues know about the subject to be communicated.

AUDIENCE INTEREST

Effective informative speaking not only involves adaptation to the knowledge level of the audience, but also selection of clarifying material which excites audience interest. Such material will add spice to what might otherwise be a dull discourse. Factor analysis can be used to determine interests as well as knowledge, but different factors will be more important, depending on whether the speaker is determining knowledge or interests. When one speaks to a women's club, he may assume that some of their hobbies are bridge, knitting, painting, and reading. The speaker would do well to draw some of the examples and analogies in his speech from these hobbies, providing he has enough knowledge to do so. Men's groups are more likely to be interested in sports and financial developments. In either case, the types of hobbies will depend to some extent on the economic and social level, and in some cases the region of the country.

Other important factors in determining interests are occupation, group affiliation, and, in some cases, nationality. If the group is homogeneous, such as a hunting club, a speech can be particularly sparkling and memorable if clarifying material utilizes this interest. What excites people also varies according to age and race, as well as level of education.

These examples of audience analysis are intended to be suggestive rather than prescriptive. As we have emphasized throughout, the amount of effort the speaker exerts to find out about the audience will vary according to how much he already knows about the specific audience. It is safe to say, however, that a speaker can never know too much about his audience. The amount of time he devotes to the effort to predict audience knowledge and interest will no doubt depend on the amount of time he has available and the importance of the communication.

THE SPEAKER'S KNOWLEDGE

At this point it should be noted that this book gives much attention to audience analysis and adaptation and little to the manner in which the speaker collects the content for his speech. This emphasis is intentional for two reasons. The first, a pedagogical reason, is that contemporary students have had considerable experience collecting data before they reach the stage at which they will read this book. Most students have written a researched report by the time they have reached fifth grade, and as they advance through the grades the number of speeches and reports they give increases each year. The second reason has to do with the circumstances under which informative speeches are given. An audience generally is willing to accept an informative discourse only from someone who is better informed on the subject than it is. For this reason it is extremely doubtful that—with the possible exception of classroom speeches—an informative speaker will give a speech on a subject which is unfamiliar to him. Of course, he may have to look up certain details or acquire additional content information in order to fill in gaps, but if he is speaking outside the context of the college speech class, it is unlikely that a speaker would be invited to give a speech on a subject about which he has little knowledge. The informative speaker is normally one who knows his subject matter. His main worry is a rhetorical one—that is, how to convey his knowledge so that it is understood by his listeners.[10]

Even students, when asked to give an informative speech for a class project, should select a topic about which they have considerable knowledge. An excellent question for the student to ask himself is, "If a group approached me with a request to tell them something they don't already know, what could I, with my present knowledge, tell them?" A speech based almost completely upon library research invariably gives itself away, especially if a question period follows the speech. Because of lack of experience with the topic, the speaker cannot relate the subject matter to other concepts and his information becomes suspect by the listeners. Since informative communication depends on the open-mindedness of the audience to the information conveyed, it is crucial that the speaker gain their confidence by demonstrating a thorough knowledge of the subject.

When students give informative speeches on subjects from the area of their specialty they are simulating the conditions under which they will present informative communications in their future occupations. Students often feel that their area of concentration will not interest a class made up of people from other areas, and therefore they think they must research topics which are of more widespread interest. This conclusion is a great mistake. Naturally, not everyone is interested in the specialty of another, but the rhetorical task is to communicate the material in such a way that many of the auditors will *become* interested. Seldom will every member of the audience be interested in the topic. A student should know this well from the fact

---

10. See the book in this series by Ronald Reid on *Developing Ideas.*

that he is not interested in every class he is required to take. However, upon taking a position after graduation, most students will communicate material in the area of their specialty. Therefore, speech training that has prepared the student for the sort of informative tasks he will perform in his profession and community is invaluable to the speaker. At the same time, the student can make his greatest contribution to his classmates by speaking on the subject about which he knows the most.

Projects

1. Try to estimate a particular class' knowledge of a subject by what you know about specific students in the class. Does the knowledge vary from person to person? What does this tell you about the nature of audiences?
2. Select a subject and think of two different audiences, one which would consider the subject informative and a second which would not. Why do you think these two audiences would react differently to the subject?
3. Give a speech on some aspect of your major interest. The speech should be on a concept of some complexity. Do you feel that you are well enough qualified to speak authoritatively to some group on the subject?
4. Write a statement two or three pages in length indicating what you estimate your audience knows about the subject of your speech. Indicate the basis upon which your estimation is made.
5. Write a paragraph explaining why you think the speech you plan to give will be accepted by the audience as informative. Is there the possibility that some in the audience will not consider it informative? What do you plan to do if two or three auditors react to your speech as if it were persuasive?

4.

STRUCTURING THE

INFORMATIVE DISCOURSE

An audience-centered approach to informative discourse has important ramifications for structuring or organizing the speech. Although the audience-centered approach to arrangement has usually been followed in *persuasion*, the theory of organization in *informative* discourse has remained message-centered.[1]

Message-centered speeches are determined by inherent relations in the subject matter. For instance, in building a model sailing boat, it is usually advisable to assemble the model before painting it. Therefore, in giving a speech on the subject, the speaker might well follow the *natural* or *inherent* order and explain the assembly process before the details of painting. Or, to take another example, the access to lakes in northern Canada is dependent on the mining and forestry industries. Therefore, if one is to talk about new roads in Canada which will increase the accessibility of lakes for fishing, he will want to point out the areas where mining is increasing, and where timber remains to be cut. Such association of ideas greatly facilitates learning.[2]

Structuring a speech according to a time sequence often is of considerable help to the person who wishes to relate and remember the various aspects of a subject; but the time sequence itself does

1. Donald C. Bryant and Karl R. Wallace, *Fundamentals of Public Speaking* (New York: Appleton-Century-Crofts, 1960), pp. 148–154.
2. See Ernest R. Hilgard, *Introduction to Psychology* (New York: Harcourt, Brace & World, Inc., 1962), pp. 336ff. Also, L. L. Clark, T. G. Lansford, and K. M. Dallenbach, "Repetition and Associative Learning," *American Journal of Psychology*, LXXIII (1960), 22–40.

not provide adaptation to the knowledge of the audience. For example, a discourse on ways of reducing the effects of aircraft sonic booms might be organized on a time sequence. But if the structure were not varied from audience to audience, the results could be disastrous; for example, the speech might be given to (1) a group of elementary teachers, and (2) a group of aerospace engineers. In each case the time sequence could be employed, but within this framework considerable adjustment would need to be made because of vast differences in audience knowledge.

The first part of this chapter will consider the traditional ways of structuring informative speeches, based on the relational (association) features of the subject matter. These traditional comments will then be followed by an analysis of audience-centered procedures suggested by programmed learning, especially *branching techniques*. Finally, suggestions will be made as to ways in which relational and audience-centered structures can be combined. We will also note the use of unusual or specialized structures.

CONTENT-INFORMED STRUCTURES

The four traditional types of informative arrangement are time, spatial, cause-effect, and topical. In a speech ordered according to a *time* sequence, one would explain computer programming step by step according to the order in which a computer program is actually prepared. Using the *spatial* order, one would explain a Gemini spacecraft by moving from place to place—for example, from bottom to top. A *cause-effect* structure might discuss a rocket motor showing first how the propulsion is produced, then discussing its effects. A *topical* arrangement divides the subject according to categories provided by the subject. In speaking about voting blocks in the United States, for instance, one might discuss the farm vote, the Polish vote, the Catholic vote, and the Jewish vote.

The traditional speech structures are built on a type of association which is fundamental to our pattern of thinking. Sometime during our elementary education, we come upon the concepts of time, space, and energy (a causal force). These aspects of our universe from then on affect the way we talk about things and become fundamental to much of our conceptualization. It is not surprising, therefore, that the divisions of a subject often fall into one of these patterns. The topical arrangement, however, reflects divisions in the specific subject under consideration. It is not the nature of the universe which forms the pattern in this case, but rather a structure emerges from within the content of the subject itself. In a sense, these topics are factors of a specific discipline. Since factors are continuously reoccurring in each discipline, a repeated framework is employed which produces certain associational values: Each time that particular subject area is discussed, these factors reappear. Different factors may be emphasized from decade to decade in any discipline, but the type of topic discussed in each remains much the same. An arrangement based on either universal relationships, e.g., time, space, or energy, or specific subject factors, e.g., topics, can provide a pattern which is helpful to the learner, since he is thereby led to form associations between the various facets of the subject.

It should be obvious that some subjects are by nature more readily divided by one of the four patterns than others. We will discuss the unique features of each.

Time sequence

Dividing a topic according to a time sequence is particularly meaningful in discussing human events or natural processes. A discourse on America's relations with Cuba or the United Nations activity in the Congo would lend itself naturally to a time sequence. With other topics, the communicator must decide whether a topical arrangement or some other type would be most helpful for the audience. The discussion of a United Nations decision, for example, could be developed either according to a time sequence or topically according to the various structures within the United Nations — such as the Security Council, the General Assembly, and the Trusteeship Council. A talk on the United States space program could be developed historically or according to topics; topically, the speaker could discuss the various projects, such as Mercury, Gemini, and Apollo. A space program speech could be both topical and chronological if the projects were discussed in the sequence of origin; it may, in fact, prove desirable to employ more than one type of arrangement in a given discourse. In discussing the laser (having to do with reconstructed light waves) one could begin by giving a short history of the considerations which went into laser development; the remainder of the speech might best be divided according to topics such as the nature of light waves, the resonant cavity, and the active material.

A time sequence need not always proceed in a forward direction. An effective speech on jazz might begin with contemporary types and then move backward, showing the occasion out of which each developed. A flashback technique might also prove effective with some types of subjects but flashback is probably more effective as an organizational principle for written discourse than oral, since it demands considerable concentration from the listener. The reader can always check back if he is puzzled by the arrangement, but the auditor cannot.

Spatial sequence

Some subjects do not lend themselves to a time sequence — for example, the composition of the human brain. Here a spatial arrangement is demanded. The spatial sequence is best employed for subjects in which space relationships provide natural divisions. These are mostly subjects that have to do with the physical world rather than human actions and events. If one were to give a speech on the city planning of Washington, D.C., he could divide the main headings according to areas of space in the city. A talk about galaxies of the universe might be structured spatially, commencing with the earth's galaxy and moving outward. A discussion of the solar system often entails a similar arrangement, beginning with the sun and moving outward from planet to planet. A spatial treatment may also contain a time factor. One could discuss the expansion of the Dupont Company as it moved from the eastern United States to the west; because of the nature of Dupont expansion, this division would also be a time sequence.

Cause-effect sequence

The cause-effect sequence has a great deal in common with the time sequence, but the two are not invariably identical. At least since David Hume, most philosophers in the Western world have considered "cause" prior in time to "effect." Aristotle and Thomas Aquinas, however, argued for a variety of causality in which cause is contemporaneous with its effect. Most people have a tendency to confuse causality with temporal sequence. A cause-effect sequence may also be a temporal sequence but it does not have to be. For instance, in discussing the 1964 racial disturbances in Cambridge, Maryland, one could employ a cause-effect sequence. He would observe the events which led the Negroes to revolt, and then review the consequences of the revolt. In this case, the causal pattern would also represent the temporal order of events. Or, a plant pathologist, discussing lawn diseases, could commence with effects on the lawn such as moldy areas, red patches, or circle discoloration. After describing these effects, which might be familiar to the audience, he would then proceed to discuss the causes. In this second instance the effect-cause pattern coincides with a reverse-chronological order.

The foregoing examples show that time and cause-effect sequences are often the same, but temporal sequence does not necessarily imply causality. A speaker may discuss the various theories of the origin of the universe in their historical sequence, but each theory is not necessarily the effect of the theory preceding it. Moreover, causality does not always imply a temporal sequence. For instance, many processes, such as the production of sound in a vibrating string, include causal patterns in which cause and effect occur contemporaneously. In explaining the operation of an atomic steam-generating plant, one would move from cause to effects in the presentation, but in the working of the plant the causes and effects are simultaneous.

Cause-effect patterns may likewise be tied in with topical divisions. An example in which time, cause-effect, and topical might occur together would be a discourse about the financial crash of 1929. The speaker could discuss the forces which contributed to the crash, then follow up with the effects of the financial conditions which ensued. In this case the cause-effect pattern would coincide with a time pattern, but it might also display a topical pattern if the speech were developed around the topics of land speculation, loans, and stock manipulation.

Topical arrangement

The two kinds of content-centered arrangements that are employed most frequently are the time and topical sequences. A topical organization is most helpful when one is concerned with the various factors that make up a greater whole. A chronological sequence may not be helpful when an overall perspective is desired. For instance, if one wishes to convey an overall view of a plant, the most efficient way probably is to divide the discussion into topics such as cells, stems, roots, and leaves. Or consider another example; architecture could be discussed by relating its history—describing the Byzantine, Romanesque, Gothic, Georgian, and Modern periods in chronological order. But the explanation would probably be more lucid if the various periods were discussed in terms of their similarities and differences. Or, in preparing a discourse on existentialism, one might divide it according to the topics: literary, religious, psychological, and philosophical. These topics would provide an overall view as to the influence which existentialism has had upon contemporary thinking. The speech would be too long if a time sequence were followed through in each of these topics.

From this examination of content-oriented structures, it becomes clear that the nature of the content will determine which organizational pattern is the most helpful. In some cases the speaker will have a choice of one or more structure types or a combination of two or more. He should carefully consider which pattern or combination will be most helpful on the particular subject and for the particular audience, and in view of the amount of time available.

AUDIENCE-ORIENTED STRUCTURES

If the content of a discourse is relatively simple for the audience (for example, a description of the signals employed by a football referee would be simple for Americans, but not for Tibetans), a content-centered structure would ordinarily suffice. If the subject is complex, however — for example, quantum mechanics — serious attention must be given to structuring the discourse so that the speaker begins at the level of the audience. As we have emphasized, much informative discourse in our time involves subject matter of considerable complexity, and there is a glaring need to structure material so that it is most easily comprehended by an audience.

Perhaps the reason why textbooks on speaking and writing do not give serious attention to audience-oriented informative structures is that we are accustomed to thinking mainly in terms of communications which are relatively simple. But attempts to clarify complex materials for those who lack information are going on about us all the time, the efforts to explain space programs being a prime example. If one purports to know something about communication, he should therefore concern himself with discourse in which the ideas are complex. If we share our cultural commitment that everyone with desire has the right to know, then we should also accept the task of finding means of communicating complex concepts in such a manner that they may be understood more readily.

THE PROGRAMMED LEARNING ANALOGY

One of the most systematic attempts to arrange informative material so as to adapt it to the audience is *programmed learning*. There are two basic types of programmed learning — the linear program and the branching program. In the linear program, the learner moves straight through the materials without any adjustment for mistakes that may indicate inadequate learning. Programs of this sort have been constructed in English grammar, mathematical set theory, and other subjects. The branching program reroutes the learner (sends him off on a branch) when it becomes apparent that he has failed to grasp certain basic concepts. Branching programs have as yet been used primarily in machine instruction and have been employed much less than the linear program, though one can find in most bookstores programmed textbooks of the branching type that deal with a variety of topics ranging from basic electronics to contract bridge.

The assumption the linear program makes is that a given audience has traits that are universal for that group. A program is set up for, say, a basic physics course for tenth-graders, and it is assumed that the structure is suitable for any tenth-grader. This approach is similar to the universal trait analysis of traditional rhetoric. However, as everyone knows, tenth-graders vary considerably in their preparedness and ability to grasp the principles of physics. The linear program can only posit the average tenth-grade audience. Therefore it has limited application if one is interested in an audience-adapted structure that takes individual differences into account. The branching type program, in contrast, accounts for these differences, and thus is the type program upon which the remainder of this discussion is based.

The task confronting one preparing an informative discourse differs in certain fundamental ways from that confronting the one who prepares a program. In the first place, a speaker does not have the time available while he is speaking to develop a topic in the systematic manner of programmed instruction. It is therefore necessary that he take whatever short cuts are permissible with a particular audience. (In presenting a series of lectures, a speaker might have a situation comparable to that of programmed learning in that much more time for lecturing is available to him.) In the second place, a speaker does not always have the homogeneous audience that most programs presuppose. The audience for a lecture I once heard on existentialism varied from first-year college students without any background in philosophy to a number of university philosophy professors. Of course, complete adaptation to such an audience is almost impossible for a speaker, but programs must ignore such wide varieties, though the purpose of branching is to make some accommodation. Finally, informative discourse normally does not permit continual testing to determine whether or not previous concepts have been mastered. Because of these differences, the application of program structuring to informative discourse is limited, but some helpful insights may be obtained by way of analogy.

Audience analysis is as crucial to programmed learning as it is to informative speaking. In linear programming, those who compose the program first decide the general type of audience for which they wish to design the program, then carefully determine the characteristics of this group. Since the program is constructed for the average student in that group, mathematical models can be employed as a means of predicting the knowledge of the audience. (When the audience becomes too varied, mathematical models are impracticable.)

Once the characteristics of the student have been determined, the program begins at the estimated level of the learner's knowledge. From that point, the structure develops by utilizing concepts which are available to the learner and unfolding new ones in the necessary order, but the content-centered patterns are always modified according to the needs of the students.

The branching method of programming is an attempt to adapt the structure of the program to *individual* learners. Whenever a student answers a fundamental question incorrectly, the program takes him by another route to review the material he has not learned adequately. This operation is more expensive than linear programming, and often requires a computer to plot the program. Further refinement of the branching technique has involved an attempt to predict the probable response of a student to the various questions raised, based on biographical data of that particular student. The student then receives an individual routing based on this prediction. A computer selects the material as the student moves along, employing probabilistic mathematical models.[3]

These mathematical models are too complicated and refined to be of much practical use to the informative speaker, but they do suggest certain general principles. In the first place, we have offered factor analysis as a method of predicting audience knowledge on a specific subject. Factor analysis is analogous in some ways to the probabilistic mathematical models of programmers. For instance, a flow chart can allow a speaker to adapt to his audience's needs much as the teaching machine adapts by the branching technique. Flow charts outline two alternative routes, with the final outcome dependent upon which alternative is selected.

By employing a flow-chart approach, the speaker can prepare ahead of time for occasions in which audience feedback indicates that the message is not getting through. When feedback gives signs of audience confusion, the speaker is prepared with an alternative course. The structure of the speech thus becomes dynamic and audience-centered, because it is constantly being modified while it is actually being given.

We ought to recognize that the branching technique suggested by the flow chart is not a completely new method of teaching. Good teachers and speakers have always gone back to needed background when they realized that their point was not getting across. But little has been suggested in speech texts for a systematic manner of pre-

3. See Richard D. Smallwood, *A Decision Structure for Teaching Machines* (Cambridge, Mass.: M.I.T. Press, 1962). Some studies, however, have been negative in regard to the advantages of branching.

paring ahead of time for this situation. Since adaptation to feedback is one of the main advantages of oral discourse, it is essential to have a concrete program for arranging adaptation in advance.

The flow-chart method

The flow-chart method enables a speaker to prepare several alternate routes for his discourse. In case one route is not clear enough, he can choose another, more detailed, one. A simple flow-chart type speech structure on the subject "How a Car Engine Works" is shown on page 48.

This chart was purposefully made very schematic for illustrative purposes. The overall structure is essentially a time sequence, but a branch, or alternative route, is provided at each number. At (1) the speaker assumes most people will have some idea about a starter, but in case anyone is puzzled the speaker will follow the route of the branch before going on to the next point concerning the spark plugs. The same sort of detours can be taken at (2), (3), (5), and (6) if needed. At (4) the material about the motor is complete. If interest is beginning to lag or the allotted time has been used up by additional explanation, the speaker can close the speech at this point by saying that the power created by the motor is transferred to the wheels. If, however, interest and time permit, he can develop (5) and (6).

The flow chart allows the speaker to prepare for audience adaptation ahead of time, but it also has a number of disadvantages. In the first place, a built-in feature which requires a holistic approach is lacking. A person who desires that his approach be holistic will no doubt employ the flow chart so as to present a total configuration, but the chart itself does not call attention to such a need. Flow charts and programmed learning tend, however, to uphold an atomistic theory of learning; therefore, their helpfulness is limited, even though they do permit individualistic adaptation. B. F. Skinner, for example, did most of the preparatory work on programmed instruction by experimenting with animals. His method was to build individual behavior patterns from specific rewards, then to join pattern to pattern: the learning model was thus accumulative, or atomistic, rather than holistic. Atomism may not be endemic to programmed instruction and flow charts, but those who have utilized these approaches have usually been atomistically oriented.

A second major difficulty with the flow chart is that the speech tends to become unwieldy if one attempts to incorporate more than the major points on the chart. Of course, a flow chart may be the best method if the speech topic is simple. In order to adapt the flow chart to

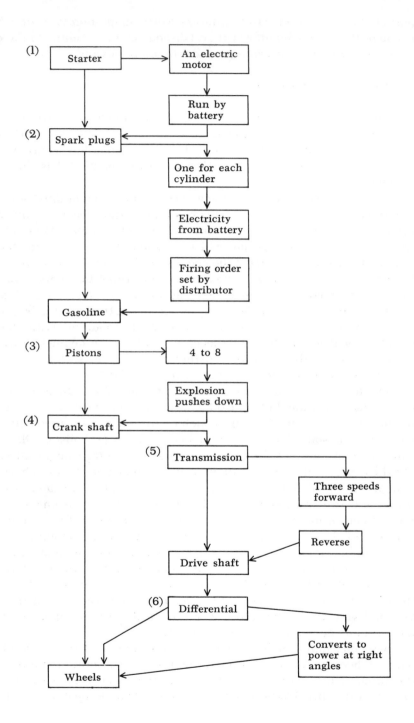

our purposes, we need some modification of the traditional structuring. At the same time our structure should use the association features of traditional patterns.

The branching outline

Borrowing from the vocabulary of programmed learning, we can call the structuring method offered here a *branching outline*. The branching outline has the characteristic features of the traditional speech outline except that it has two columns. The left-hand column follows the traditional content-centered type of structure; hence it provides a holistic and associative configuration and highlights the main points of the subject. The right-hand column contains material which can be interjected in case audience feedback indicates lack of comprehension or special interest in the point being made. At this point it should be noted that in spite of some disenchantment with the ability of a speaker to determine audience thinking from facial expressions, psychological studies show that the emotions of others can be predicted with considerable accuracy from facial expressions.[4] The right-hand column will also reflect the general level of the audience. In this sort of outline, both the associative advantages of the traditional structures and the audience-adaptive features of the flow chart are retained, and the inherent weaknesses in both are overcome.

Experienced speakers often employ traditional outlines in an adaptive way by outlining a speech as thoroughly as possible, then passing over material which audience feedback indicates is not needed. Branching outlines have the advantage over the thorough outline, however, in that they compel the speaker to give more detailed attention *before the speech gets underway* to contingencies which may require adaptation. Furthermore, a branching outline permits readier adaptation to a larger range of audiences than does a traditional outline, especially when the speaker must adapt to a more specialized audience than he had anticipated.

The more complex the topic and the longer the speech, the more helpful the branching outline becomes; the technique would not be advantageous if the speech were less than six minutes long: in a speech that short, it is difficult to deviate from the prepared statement, although in preparing a branching outline the speaker would be reminded of the need to adapt to his audience.

An example of a branching outline on the subject "The Expanding Universe" follows:

4. See William W. Lambert and Wallace E. Lambert, *Social Psychology* (Englewood Cliffs, N.J.: Prentice-Hall, Inc., 1964), pp. 28ff.

A BRANCHING OUTLINE

"THE EXPANDING UNIVERSE"

Introduction: As scientists report the data from space exploration we are impressed by the vastness of the universe. We have no doubt wondered how far out the universe goes—whether it is infinite or bounded. The contemporary view is that our universe is expanding; that it is a finite universe, yet unbounded. What are the implications of this sort of universe? Perhaps the answer can be found by examining certain historical theories.

REGULAR OUTLINE	BRANCHING

I. The Ancient Views
  A. Aristotle's universe
    1. Finite
    2. Static, neither expanding nor contracting
    3. Matter eternal, neither increasing nor decreasing
    4. Contrasts with the Judaeo-Christian concept of the universe
	A.
	  4.
	    a. The Judaeo-Christian view of creation *ex nihilo*
	      (1) Meaning of *ex nihilo*—"from nothing"
	      (2) God, not matter, eternal, He created matter from nothing
	      (3) The Judaeo-Christian universe is therefore finite
	    b. An expanding universe?
	      (1) View of some theologians that God created only once
	      (2) View of others that he continues to create, hence an expanding universe
	      (3) Biblical support for the latter view

B. Lucretius' universe
  1. Infinite
  2. Consists of atoms and
    space
    a. Number of atoms in-
      finite

B.
  2.
    a.
      (1) *Atom* in Greek—
         "uncutable"
      (2) Bodies solid, not
         firm by energy as
         in physics

    b. Movement possible
      because of space
    c. Change possible be-
      cause of movement
  3. Number of atoms con-
    stant—none created or
    destroyed
  4. Universe infinite— neither
    expands nor contracts

II. Modern Theories
  A. Aristotle's finite universe
    accepted, but its static na-
    ture rejected
  B. Albert Einstein's view
    1. Proposed a static
      universe in 1917
    2. Universe finite yet un-
      bounded
    3. Such a universe possible
      if space is curved

B.
  3.
    a. View held by Einstein
      that lines of space are
      curved
    b. Contrasts with the
      straight line of Eu-
      clidean geometry
    c. View held by Einstein
      that universe is static
      (1) Does not expand
         because of the
         curving back
      (2) Yet unbounded

4. Universe static because of curved space
C. The Lemaître-Eddington universe
   1. Universe originally a static Einstein type
   2. Now, however, expanding
   3. Finite
   4. Material in it becoming less dense because of expansion
D. The Steady-State Theory

   D. Reason for the name steady-state—density of matter in the universe remains steady in spite of expansion because of new creation from nothing

   1. Set forth by Herman Bondi, T. Gold, and Fred Hoyle
   2. Universe expanding
   3. Density remains same due to creation from nothing

   3.
   a. Proposed by William H. McCrea that the new creation takes place deep in the heart of galaxies in the form of new atoms
   b. Older steady-state view of Hoyle, et al., that matter is created in the lonely spaces of the universe

---

Conclusion: The modern physicist still accepts Aristotle's finite universe, but the modern universe is an expanding one. The Eddington theory is currently the most popular, but the steady-state view commands considerable interest. Regardless, the universe is still so vast that we need not weep with Alexander for the lack of worlds to conquer.

First, we need to say something about the audience for which this speech is intended. The speaker is a physics major—his audience is a speech class. Many of the students are majors in the sciences, though a few liberal arts students are present, and most are males. With this audience, the speaker estimates that a general understanding of the nature of the universe will prevail, but that few, if any in the audience, will have studied the subject systematically.

The introduction of the speech locates the topic at the point at which audience knowledge and interest probably converge. This establishes a common ground. The basic structure is the traditional time sequence, employed here because it permits the speaker to move from the fairly simple early views to the more complex modern ones, although students without a background in the ancients may have difficulty even with the early views. These students must attain a basic knowledge of the ancients in order to understand the presuppositions which underpin modern theories. To achieve this, the time sequence in some measure incorporates into the outline the adaptive principle of programmed learning. The time sequence also provides a total configuration to which auditors can relate the details presented.

Because of the difficulty of the concepts in this speech, the speaker can predict that certain spots will be troublesome. The branching column is his way of being prepared when audience feedback indicates the need for additional material: the speaker is prepared to amplify his comments at each branching point.

The first point at which the speaker predicts difficulty is the reference to the Judaeo-Christian view of creation. The material in the branch is not included in the regular part of the outline, since the listeners may understand the religious view or may not be interested in it. If feedback indicates lack of understanding or heightened interest at this point, the speaker is prepared to expand. The second branch concerns Lucretius' view of the atom. On this point, the speaker may find an expression of surprise that an ancient held such a modern view of the atomic composition of matter. If surprise is evident, the speaker is prepared to go into more detail concerning the differences. The reasons why curved space implies a finite universe may not be clear when the idea is suggested. Those with a background in mathematics or physics will not have any difficulty comprehending, but the others might. Furthermore, the steady-state theory may be mistaken for a static theory of the universe. If feedback indicates difficulty, the speaker is prepared to define what is meant by *steady-state*. Finally, interest may be aroused concerning the place in which new matter is created. The branch for the view of McCrea will provide further information on this subject. Because of the complexity of this speech, the place of creation in the steady-state theory should be left out, unless the audience indicates interest, since the presentation of too much material will only result in confusion.

The advantages of the branching outline as a means of preparing adaptation in advance should now be clear. Some of the traditional outline approaches are retained, but in such a way as to permit adaptation to the audience. Speakers have long needed a manner of preparing for audience adaptation in advance. Perhaps the branching method suggested here is a feasible contribution to that end.

CREATIVE STRUCTURES

Before concluding our remarks about structure, we should make some observations on the psychological soundness of creative patterns of organization. These patterns depend for the most part on (1) natural or habitual relations, (2) famous statements, and (3) humor or—specifically—play on words.

A structure which builds on familiar objects or habitual relationships can be striking. Some years ago I heard a speaker discuss the characteristics of good citizenship. He used the keys on his key ring to introduce his main headings, which were the home, the office, the church, and the service club. As each main point was brought up, he separated a different key on his key ring. A well-known statement can also serve as a creative structure. In the biography of a well-known minister, one author employed as his chapter headings a phrase from the Scriptures: I. "From These Roots" II. "First the Blade" III. "Then the Ear" IV. "Then the Full Grain in the Ear."[5] A play on words to produce humor can also give a speech structure a creative twist. In his book *The Great Crash, 1929*, John K. Galbraith employed this technique in some of his chapter headings. Included were: "In Goodman, Sachs We Trust," "Something Should Be Done," and "The Twilight of Illusion."

These creative structures should not be cultivated for their own sake—to do so encourages artificiality. They should be utilized only when they call attention to the content of the speech rather than away from it. One of the principles of learning theory is that we retain longer that which is particularly striking.[6] Since retention is often a goal of informative discourse, a striking effect may be very helpful. If adaptation to the audience (the most important consideration) can be combined with a striking effect, the speech will have the greatest chance of being effective. The more learning principles the speaker utilizes in his informative communication, the greater should be the amount of learning which results.

Projects

1. Select a topic that you can outline according to all four classical methods. Can you think of an appropriate audience for each one of these methods?

5. Louis Cochran, *The Fool of God* (New York: Duell, Sloan & Pearce, 1958).
6. Sarnoff A. Mednick, *Learning* (Englewood Cliffs, N.J.: Prentice-Hall, Inc., 1964), pp. 68ff.

2. Prepare a branch outline for a speech in which you present an idea of some complexity. The speech should be ten to fifteen minutes in length. Make the regular part of the outline first, then ask yourself which parts of the outline may require further elaboration. Use the branching part of your outline to clarify these spots.
3. Visit a programmed-learning center and learn how the branching technique is employed on teaching machines.
4. Look at a programmed text and see how the organization unfolds. How might you improve the structure to make it easier for you to understand?
5. Write a statement describing one of your professors' method of outlining his lectures. Does he employ both associative and adaptive features? Does he branch in response to a question, or an indication that someone does not understand what he is talking about?

5.

THE LANGUAGE OF

INFORMATIVE DISCOURSE

Clarity of language is an important factor in the effective communication of information. Ideas must be stated distinctly if they are to be understood by listeners. Distinctness has to do partly with overall structure and such techniques as examples and analogies; but it also has to do with word order, accuracy of vocabulary, explanation of technical terms, and the concreteness of language. If audiences differ and if individuals in audiences are not all the same in experience and outlook, then we cannot follow inflexible rules for improving clarity. Rather, we must take into account differing subjects and audiences, remembering that what is *clear* will differ from one situation to another. The characteristics of clear statement are: (1) accuracy, (2) economy, and (3) specificity.

ACCURACY

If ideas are to be distinct, words must be employed accurately; but there can be no fast set of rules outlining the nature of accurate language. What is accurate language for laymen may not be accurate for specialists. Communication intended for the layman must use popular language, while the language for the specialist should be technical for the sake of accuracy. Popular language is usually less precise than technical language and does not express ideas as succinctly.

We may assume that the directions taken from the back of a bag of patching plaster presuppose an audience that requires popular language. The directions from "Evans Patching Plaster" state:

> For ordinary patching work, Evans Patching Plaster should be mixed in proportions of approximately one pint of cold water to two pounds of plaster. This however, may be varied to some extent, as conditions warrant.
>
> In a clean non-absorbent container, place the required amount of cold water, to which Evans Patching Plaster should be added. Allow to stand for three minutes before mixing. Then, slowly stir until the plaster has entirely absorbed all the water and is of a uniformly smooth consistency. It is then ready for use.

The words in these directions are as precise as they could be for the average layman. For those accustomed to mixing plaster, the same directions may be stated more succinctly, though not with any appreciable increase in technical language (since little is available):

> Mix Evans Patching Plaster in proportions of approximately 1:2. Pour in cold water first and then add the plaster. Allow three minutes to elapse before stirring, then mix until homogenized.

The experienced painter or plasterer should know whether or not his patching task were "ordinary." He could be given proportions rather than weights and measures because he is familiar with proportion arrangements. He would not need to be told about the type or cleanliness of the container or about rapidity of mixing. Even though there is little technical language in this case, the experienced plasterer could understand much more succinct and economical directions than could the layman.

Television repair, on the other hand, is an area where highly technical language can be employed. The following statement is taken from a manual titled *Television Analyzing Simplified.* In the introduction, the author offers the work as helpful "irrespective of the skill of the man using the ANALYST, whether he be an experienced technician or a beginner."[1] If he is a beginner, however, he would have to learn some of the vocabulary. Some of it he would get by reading the book:

> If the synchronization of the picture did not become intermittent, but remained in sync under all conditions, this would tell us that

1. Milton S. Kiver, *Television Analyzing Simplified* (Chicago: Van Nostrand, 1960), p. iii.

from the plate of the sync amplifier tube into the oscillator there was no trouble. We would now shift our point sync injection to the grid of the 6BF6 sync amplifier. At this point we would have to reverse the phase of the sync signal to allow for the phase inversion of the sync amplifier tube and also to reduce the level of the sync signal to take into account the gain of this stage.[2]

The accuracy of the language in this case results from the use of technical terms which have precise meaning for the technician. An attempt to write the same instructions in popular language would entail lengthier explanations and probably less precision. The first sentence alone, if rewritten for a lay audience would read something like this:

If the images on the television screen are continuous and remain in proper form under all conditions, the devices having to do with synchronization are functioning properly. The synchronization tube apprehends the synchronization impulse transmitted by the station, and directs the emission of electrons at the surface of the picture tube so that they are distributed in precisely the same order as arranged by the television camera. This tells us that from the plate (that is, the collector of electrons in the tube) of the synchronization amplifier tube into the oscillator (the device which reverses the current so as to keep the electrons flowing) there is no trouble.

In order to make this material understandable to the person without proper background knowledge, familiar language must be used. The result is that although the statement is accurate, it is less precise and economical than if written for the technician.[3]

However, when the message to be conveyed is not one of instructions, as in the two cases cited, but of explication of complex theories, the precision of language acquires additional features. In the case of instructions, the important nouns have observable referents. In the statement about plaster, the nouns and adjectives "pint," "cold water," "two pounds," "clean non-absorbent," and "three minutes," may be perceived by the senses in some manner or another. The same is the case in the statement about television with such words as "picture," "intermittent," "plate," and "sync amplifier tube." In the case of the television terms, anyone without prior instruction might have difficulty connecting the names with their referents, but all the

2. *Ibid.*, p. 105.
3. A fuller treatment of this topic from a slightly different viewpoint appears in Hubert G. Alexander's book in this series, *Meaning in Language.*

nouns and adjectives in this passage can be located in the observable world. When nouns refer to observable properties or objects, language requires less prior orientation. Some communication, however, involves language in which the nouns and adjectives do not refer to sensed properties; then the problem of accuracy is more complicated.

One subject in which some of the technical language is not grounded in sense objects is certain types of philosophy. The following statement of Charles Peirce displays language of this sort.

> When Descartes set about the reconstruction of philosophy, his first step was to (theoretically) permit skepticism and to discard the practice of the schoolmen of looking to authority as the ultimate source of truth. . . . Self-consciousness was to furnish us with our fundamental truths, and to decide what was agreeable to reason. But since, evidently, not all ideas are true, he was led to note, as the first condition of infallibility, that they must be clear.[4]

The important nouns here, such as "philosophy," "skepticism," "schoolmen," "ultimate," "truth," and "infallibility" do not refer to objects or properties which are located in the world of empirical perception. Accuracy in this case therefore is *not* judged by how well the language describes objects in the perceivable world, but by how well the language points to concepts which are framed by men and located in language itself. Of course, some conceptual words appear even in the plaster mixing directions, but they are not the important nouns and adjectives.

Theories of language

The theory of language which states that all words refer to perceptible properties is called *the referent theory of language*. This theory is clearly inadequate, even in the case of those subjects in which the important nouns and adjectives do have sensed referents; for even in simple directions there are words that do not have such referents, such as *for, should, however*, and *would*;[5] and in certain types of discourse, referent language is infrequent. As Alston writes:

> Speech does not consist of producing a sequence of labels, each of which is attached to something in "the world." Some of the meaningful components of the sentences we use to talk about the

4. *Philosophical Writings of Peirce*, ed. Justus Buchler (New York: Dover Publications, Inc., 1955), p. 24.
5. This point is discussed more fully by Theodore Clevenger, Jr., and Jack Matthews in *The Speech Communication Process*, another book in this series.

world can be connected in semantically important ways to distinguishable components of the world, but others cannot.[6]

If we accept Alston's view, then what we say about language accuracy will differ from one discourse to another, depending upon the amount of referent language which the discourse contains.

Another way of dealing with the problem of referent and nonreferent language is to say that nonreferent language has no meaning. This was the position taken by a group of philosophers called *logical positivists* who, in turn, influenced Alfred Korzybski and, through him, the movement known as *general semantics*.[7] The difficulty with the logical positivist view of language, as Susanne Langer has aptly observed, is that positivists granted the validity of mathematics, even though it is a form of language for which no objects can be discovered in the perceived world.[8] Few philosophers these days deny meaning to concepts for which no object can be discovered. Therefore, if we are going to understand the problem of clarity in such language, we need to consider these conceptual words from the standpoint of accuracy.

Conceptual language

Conceptual language is of two sorts—that which proceeds metaphorically from what can be sensed, and that in which the concepts can be located only in the words themselves.

Let us again refer to television repair: for the most part, the repairman works with terms which have concrete referents in the set. But if he attempted to explain how pictures are transmitted through the air, he would have to describe radio waves, which do not have a concrete referent. To be sure, their effects can be sensed; but the observable effects (a picture or sound) tell us little about the nature of the waves themselves. Because radio waves cannot be observed, the language to describe them must therefore be metaphorical in comparison to something that can be sensed directly, such as ocean waves. Accuracy in this case is judged by how precisely the metaphorical language reflects the real object which is unseen. In this case, *wave* seems to be the most exact metaphor possible. In the case of the production of sound waves in the human larynx, two words have been employed for the vibrators: *cords* and *folds*. Many anato-

6. William P. Alston, *Philosophy of Language* (Englewood Cliffs, N.J.: Prentice-Hall, Inc., 1964), p. 19.

7. Alfred Korzybski, *Science and Sanity* (Lancaster, Pa.: Science Press, 1941), pp. 412ff. Cf. Wendell Johnson, "Scientific Writing: An Introduction to General Semantics," in Shaw, *A Complete Course in Freshman English* (New York: Harper & Brothers, 1955), pp. 256–257.

8. Susanne K. Langer, *Philosophy in a New Key* (New York: Mentor Books, 1958), p. 28.

mists have argued that the term *cords* is misleading; they declare that *folds* is the more accurate of the two terms, because it provides the best description. Much of our language is metaphorical in precisely this manner; hence accuracy must take into account metaphorical conceptualization.[9] Language can never be completely precise; a degree of ambiguity is always present.[10] Such an admission is highly significant for anyone who intends to set up rules about language accuracy.

The concern with precision in language, at least from a referent standpoint, is highest in the natural sciences; when we leave the natural sciences, ambiguity increases, even though the speaker or writer may contend that his language is precise. For example, Wendell Johnson contends that the accuracy of the terms *conservative*, *liberal*, and *radical* can be measured scientifically; hence ambiguity is reduced by the use of percentages. His method is to ask a number of people to use one of these terms to describe various political personalities. The percentage of agreement in the results is then used as a measure of how precise or ambiguous the word is, so that even though the word may be ambiguous, its degree of ambiguity is measured.[11] While Johnson's program may discover something of the manner in which different people use words, it doesn't tell *why* they use them as they do. Four people might label Franklin D. Roosevelt a radical, yet each may define the word differently. Let us assume, for example, that the four are (1) a college professor, (2) an exile from Hungary, (3) a newspaper publisher, and (4) a Texas rancher. It is conceivable that in each case the reason for calling Roosevelt a radical would be entirely different. Conceptual words in philosophy and theology also pose similar problems. What one philosopher means by the word *cause* may not be what another means. The word *atonement* may mean one concept to a given theologian and something quite different to another.

Besides failing to define words' meanings, Johnson's program does not work because it relies on the referent theory of language, which we have already found to be unsatisfactory (see page 59).

Accuracy and informative speaking

We have raised these scientific and philosophical questions not for their own sake, but because they enter in a very tangible way the

9. An interesting discussion of this point may be found in I. A. Richards, *The Philosophy of Rhetoric* (New York: Oxford University Press, Inc., 1936), p. 91.
10. Arguments supporting the contention that language, even in scientific propositions, is never fully precise, may be found in *Philosophical Writings of Peirce*, ed. Justus Buchler (New York: Dover Publications, Inc., 1955), pp. 374, 376.
11. Wendell Johnson, *People in Quandaries* (New York: Harper & Brothers, 1946), pp. 507ff.

task of the informative speaker. What implication does the ambiguity of language have for the communicator? One popular conclusion is that language precision is impossible, that we never really manage to communicate with one another in an authentic way. Existentialists, in particular, dwell upon the ambiguity of language and the difficulty of communication.[12] In the view of some existentialists, authentic communication is systematically impossible, and therefore rules for accuracy are worthless. But in light of our experience in social intercourse, it appears more reasonable to believe that some communication gets through despite such pessimism, especially when words have the same meaning for the communicator and his audience.[13] Nevertheless, communication *is* difficult. It is unrealistic to believe that whenever someone speaks, whoever hears will understand what he says. There is likely to be some misunderstanding even when the speaker prepares his speech for a specific audience.

We return, therefore, to a fundamental thesis of this book: that in order to communicate effectively, a speaker must consider his audience as individuals. It is only when individuals in a specific audience understand words in the same manner as the speaker that he can communicate accurately. As J. Bronowski has stated, "No explicit statement, no communicable language can formulate generalizations which are more precise than the common agreements between those who use them."[14] Language that is precise according to some supposedly absolute, content-centered criteria may convey little to an audience that does not share the speaker's definitions of the language he uses.

Achieving accuracy in discourse

We are now prepared to offer advice as to ways in which the language of informative discourse may be made more accurate. Accuracy will be defined differently in different speaking situations.

If one is giving technical instructions to a nontechnical audience, precise language would be that which uses words that are in common use to describe the objects being discussed. Because the language is popular rather than technical, a relatively large number of words may be required. If the communication is to a group of technicians, on the

12. See Søren Kierkegaard, *The Point of View for My Work as An Author,* trans. Walter Lowrie (New York: Harper Torchbooks, 1962), pp. 10ff. Cf. Martin Heidegger, *Being and Time,* trans. John Macquarrie (London: S.C.M. Press, 1964), pp. 188–224, and Jean Paul Sartre, *What Is Literature?* trans. Bernard Frechtman (New York: Washington Square Press, 1965), pp. 16ff.
13. For philosophical support of this view see Ludwig Wittgenstein, *Philosophical Investigations* (New York: The Macmillan Company, 1953).
14. J. Bronowski, *The Common Sense of Science* (New York: Vintage Books, Inc., n. d.), p. 116.

other hand, the accuracy is enhanced by the use of technical words. Choice of these words will depend on the knowledge of the audience and how helpful the words are to their understanding the material. By the use of technical vocabulary, the communication can be made more precise with fewer words.

If the discussion has to do with physical properties which cannot be sensed, the language will, of necessity, be metaphorical. If the audience is a popular, or nontechnical, one, accuracy of language is judged by the precision with which the words depict the phenomenon. An engineer might, in talking to a lay audience about sonic booms, refer to the *wall of pressure* which builds up in front of the wing of the plane. Perhaps *compressed wave of air* would be more precise because it better describes the actual occurence; but neither of these phrases would be precise for a technician. He would prefer rather to speak of the pounds of air pressure per cubic inch at varying altitudes. His language is still metaphorical, but it is more accurate.

In language for which there is no concrete referent, accuracy is possible, but through different means. In this case, the meaning of words depends solely on speaker-audience agreements, for words cannot be explained merely by pointing to some object. The formula for precision is thus a continual awareness of the manner in which people from different disciplines and cultural groups employ words; this can only emerge from frequent contact with these persons or groups of persons. When it is impossible for a person to say what he wishes to say employing his audience's terminology, he sets forth the meaning he is conferring on his words as he goes along. In a recent speech a Hindu explained the Hinduism of south India to a group from the Jewish and Christian faiths. The terms employed by the Hindu were, for the most part, those used in Judaeo-Christian theology. What these terms mean in Hindu though, however, is sometimes radically different. In some cases the speaker noted these differences, but in others he did not. The result was that many in the audience became confused, a fact which became obvious in the question period.[15]

A few examples will indicate ways in which those who communicate may acquire sensitivity to the manner in which words are employed. The word *rhetoric* has already been introduced in this book, and it is a word with various meanings, depending on the group by which it is used. Certain speech teachers, when using the word *rhetoric*, have in mind the persuasion found in public speeches. Philosophers often confer perjorative power on the word and by it mean

15. More extended discussions of language, some of which concern accuracy, may be found in Alston, *Philosophy of Language* (Englewood Cliffs, N.J.: Prentice-Hall, Inc., 1964); J. B. Carroll, *The Study of Language* (Cambridge, Mass.: Harvard University Press, 1953); S. Ullmann, *Semantics: An Introduction to the Science of Meaning* (New York: Barnes & Noble, Inc., 1962).

"verbal manipulation." Those who teach writing often use the word to mean "style." If a speaker is to use the word *rhetoric* accurately, he must be aware of how his particular audience uses the word. If he means something different by the word, and if he hopes to communicate, he must point out what *he* means in contrast with what *they* mean.

Let us consider another example: the term *atonement* is employed by most Christian theologians, but Gustaf Aulèn finds at least three different ways in which the word is employed. The first he calls the *dramatic* theory, in which Christ's work is seen as dramatic warfare against the forces of evil. The second is the *objective* theory, which affirms that God's honor was satisfied in the death of Christ in an objective way. The third is the *subjective* theory, which affirms that Christ's death is a moving demonstration of forgiving love.[16] Precision in the use of the word *atonement* thus requires an awareness of what the word means to the particular audience to which one is speaking.

Accuracy of language is not haphazard; an understanding of the nature of language and attention to the manner in which different people use words will enable the speaker to increase accuracy when he attempts to talk with others.

ECONOMY

Almost everyone has had the experience of receiving either incomplete or excessive directions. Proper use of an adequate number of words is called *economy of language*. Economy, as well as accuracy, depends on the nature of the subject matter and the audience to whom a message is directed. The economy of language in expressing simple messages differs from that in expressing ideas that are more complex. Good instructions for assembling a bicycle tell the reader exactly what he needs to know in as few words as possible. Little technical knowledge can be assumed, however; therefore the instructions cannot be too concise. As the subject matter becomes more complex, explanations designed for a popular audience must be made more elaborate. If the audience has technical training, however, as it would in the case of directions for television repair, there is a proportionate reduction, through the use of technical terms, of the number of words needed. In some cases, however, the communicator may choose to give additional information in the time that is saved by the use of technical language. This additional information is not given to

16. Gustaf Aulèn, *Christus Victor* (New York: The Macmillan Company, 1931).

the layman since it would only confuse him. The point of these observations is that standards of economy are difficult to establish through a word-count method. The only viable word-count standard would be one which would account for the complexity of the subject matter and audience sophistication, and then set up differing counts for a variety of subjects and audiences.

We have observed that as specialization increases, the amount of information per word likewise increases. If a geneticist is talking to a group of biochemists about the manner in which chemicals control inheritance, he may use the abbreviation *DNA*, and his audience will know immediately what he means. If he is speaking to a Kiwanis Club on the same subject, however, he will need to explain that DNA stands for deoxyribonucleic acid, and discuss briefly its composition and properties. In other words, as we discovered in our discussion of accuracy, the technician has a shorthand system of communicating with other technicians. For him, economical language consists of fewer words than it does for someone communicating with a layman.

In subjects such as philosophy and theology, economy of language often depends, like accuracy, upon whether an audience is inclined to use vocabulary in the same manner as the speaker. If one is fairly sure that he is using words in the same way that his audience does, he can express his ideas in fewer words than if they use words differently. If one is a member of some continuing discussion group, such as a book club, a dorm bull-session group, or a scholarly society, he eventually knows what different members of the group mean by different words. If the reading group has discussed Aristotle's *Nicomachaean Ethics*, the speaker can use the words *happiness, the mean,* and *teleology,* and members will understand what he means. If the audience has not read the *Ethics*, however, the speaker must explain his vocabulary. Or take the case of a bull session in which considerable time has been spent discussing religion. Suppose that the group has talked about Thomas Aquinas' five ways of proving the existence of God. If, in a later discussion, someone wishes to refer to one of the *ways* he can simply mention the *third way*, and his listeners will know what he is talking about. If he is speaking to another group, however (for example, the youth fellowship of his home church), he cannot assume that they will know what he means by the *third way*, since they likely have not discussed the Thomistic proofs, so he will find it necessary to explain the argument in some detail.

Inasmuch as the economy of language depends on the nature of the subject and the understanding of the audience, one must take these factors into account when determining what economy is for a particular speech. Likewise, one who examines a message to determine the economy of language cannot judge it on the basis of some external criterion such as word count. He can make a judgment only after knowing something about the subject, the purpose of the speaker, and the nature of the audience for which the message was intended.

SPECIFICITY

Specificity of language has to do with the use of words which refer to particular, as opposed to general, ideas and objects. However, specificity cannot be determined by adding up the words which refer to individual things or ideas. Like accuracy and economy, specificity will depend on the nature of the subject and the understanding of the audience. The importance of specificity to effective clarification is that it assists the listener by locating the concept or object *within the range of his experience.* The psychological principle of association suggests that specificity should be helpful to understanding, since through specific language the listener can associate the new ideas being expressed with those with which he is already familiar. The audience is the most important consideration in determining how much or how little specificity is helpful. In this chapter, specificity means that which has to do with language rather than examples (which are discussed in the next chapter under a different heading). If the audience has had considerable experience with the subject matter, the listeners can supply the specificity for themselves as the speaker moves along. If, however, the audience has had little contact with the subject under discussion, greater amounts of specific language are necessary. The *nature* of the specificity will likewise depend on the experiences of the auditors. Language which is specific to a college-trained audience may be quite abstract to an audience without such education, and certain terms which are specific to mechanics or farmers may be abstract to audiences without experience in mechanics or farming.

Specific language usually employs concrete nouns, adverbs, and adjectives. E. C. Large, a plant pathologist, has written a book in which he attempts to discuss plant diseases and treatment in such a manner that it can be understood by those unfamiliar with the subject. One of the means through which he attempts to achieve this clarification is the use of specific language. In discussing the development of the chemical-control industry, he writes:

> The peach trees of the United States, like the apple and also the citrus trees, were terribly infested by San Jose Scale insects. These creatures, rather like minute limpets, an eighth of an inch

in diameter, clung fast in great numbers to the twigs and branches, whose juices they sucked. The pest had first claimed attention in the Santa Clara Valley, about 1870, and it had spread throughout California and into the eastern States until thousands of orchards were alive with it. Various control measures were tried with greater or less success, and some enterprising growers in California have taken to spraying their trees in the winter with a sheep-dip, of which a sample had been sent to one of their number by a friend in Australia, circa 1881. The sheep-dip was made by boiling sulphur with lime, and so effective was it against the Scale insects on peach trees that it was already in common use in California by 1885.[17]

This statement is filled with a number of specific words which, if within the experience of the reader, are very helpful. The statement could be rewritten in general terms as follows:

A new chemical industry concerned with control of plant disease was initiated in California in the late nineteenth century. Peach trees became diseased in California and farmers had little success in combatting the disease. Finally, a farmer received from an Australian friend some sheep-dip which was found to be extremely effective in controlling the small insects. Manufacturing of the sheep-dip was thus commenced and was in common use in 1885.

The revised statement is obviously more economical and says essentially as much as the original. By Large's more specific statement, however, the audience is likely to learn more and be more interested, providing they know something about California, peach trees, and sheep-dip. Some audiences would be assisted little by such specificity. A person who has lived all his life on the East Side of Manhattan would know little about peach trees and sheep-dip. In this case the specific language would probably prove a hindrance rather than a help.

To cite another case, those who attempt to read Hebrew poetry often find it difficult because the language is specific with regard to ancient cities, customs, and nations. The specificity of the poetry thus hinders comprehension until one has immersed himself in ancient Near Eastern studies.

In some cases, generality may be preferable for the specialist audience as well as for the layman. Large's specificity might be in-

17. E. C. Large, *The Advance of the Fungi* (New York: Dover Publications, Inc., 1962), p. 324.

teresting to a person trained in plant pathology, but unless it included such things as technical names for the disease, and the chemical properties of the sheep-dip, it would probably not be as helpful as a very general description. With a general description, the listener's own knowledge would supply the specifics, as we saw in the case of the patching-cement directions (see page 57). The following passage, taken from F. C. Copleston's *Aquinas*, also illustrates this situation: the apparently general language is quite specific enough for the reader who has some philosophical training.

> Other objections against the medieval metaphysicians are so closely connected with a particular philosophical system that they cannot easily be handled in a short work devoted to the system of another philosopher. If, for example, one accepts the Kantian philosophy, one will necessarily consider that the notion of the medieval metaphysicians that they could obtain knowledge of metaphysical reflection was misguided.[18]

Nouns which refer to concepts rather than objects or properties are interpreted as specific by those who know the concepts. Others may be aware that the meaning is not general, but the language will be abstract to them because of their unfamiliarity with the concepts to which it refers.

If a communicator desires to use specific language, he should first determine what is specificity for the subject matter at hand. Then he must turn to the audience and decide what words will be specific for them in view of their particular understanding of the subject.

TWO OTHER ASPECTS OF CLARITY

Syntax

The manner in which words are arranged in thought patterns (or syntax) often affects clarity. Compound sentences, especially when expressed in a passive voice, make a message difficult to comprehend, and this problem is made greater when the communication is oral. A style labeled *heavy Germanic* has these characteristics, the difficulty of which is illustrated by a statement from Edmund Husserl's *Cartesian Meditations*. Husserl's style of writing makes his ideas difficult to comprehend, even if one is a professional philosopher.

18. F. C. Copleston, *Aquinas* (London: Penguin Books, Inc., 1957), p. 18.

Though each singly selected type is thus elevated from its milieu within the empirically factual transcendental ego into the pure eidetic sphere, the intentional out horizons pointing to its uncoverable connexus within the ego do not vanish; only this *nexus-horizon itself becomes eidetic.* In other words: With each eidetically pure type we find ourselves, not indeed inside the de facto ego, but *inside an eidos ego;* and constitution of one actually pure possibility among others carries with it implicity, as its out horizon a *purely possible* ego, a pure possibility-variant of my *de facto* ego.[19]

This passage has been translated from the German, but the syntax is essentially the same as that of the German. Of course, the complexity of the syntax with which the audience can cope depends on their level of education and the complexity of the ideas with which they are accustomed to working. Therefore, no general rule pertaining to the complexity of syntax may be presented. Generally speaking, however, oral communication requires greater syntactical simplicity than does written communication, since comprehension must be immediate.

Simplicity

Simplicity is often mentioned as an attribute of effective language. Simplicity normally means the use of short sentences with Anglo-Saxon words of few syllables. No doubt, simple language is valuable in some cases, but the manner in which it enhances clarification depends again on the nature of the subject and the audience.

In spite of claims to the contrary, simple language does not always make ideas easy to comprehend, nor is it always the most helpful language. The book in the New Testament which contains the simplest language, both in the Greek and in English translation, is the Gospel of John. But in spite of the simplicity of its language, the concepts are difficult and often misunderstood, sometimes because the simplicity is misleading. At the turn of the nineteenth century, New Testament scholars argued that in the phrase, "In the beginning was the Word," *word (logos* in Greek) meant the same as the *logos* principle in Stoic philosophy. Somewhat later, however, scholars pointed out that the Gospel contained the statement, "And the Word became flesh and dwelt among us," a meaning incompatible with the Stoic view. *Logos* was one of the most simple and frequent words in the Greek vocabulary, but the very fact of its simplicity gave rise to misunderstanding rather than clarification.

19. Edmund Husserl, *Cartesian Meditations,* trans. Dorion Cairns (The Hague: Martinus Nijhoff, 1960), p. 71.

Even though the Gospel of John is not easy to understand, it might well have an excellent rating according to a readability scale designed by Rudolph Flesch. Flesch's scale classifies a communication by the number of words above four syllables and words of non-Anglo-Saxon origins it contains and by its sentence lengths.[20] As these factors increase, according to Flesch, readability decreases. The Flesch approach to simplicity has value for those who communicate simple ideas to popular audiences; it is obvious from reading Flesch's work that the material he works with is fairly simple. He does not concern himself, at least in his examples, with ideas of any complexity. It is obvious, however, that this method would be inadequate in dealing with ideas of any complexity. In order to convey difficult ideas, the speaker must help the audience learn the necessarily complex vocabulary. For instance, the word *catalyst* is not in popular vocabulary, but it is much easier to explain the meaning of the term than it is to describe certain chemical reactions without it. The same is true of *de facto recognition*, terminology employed in international politics.

When specialists communicate with other specialists, simple language may hinder clarification. Specialists can convey much more information and convey it more accurately when they employ technical terms. It is obvious that if an idea is simple, an attempt to make it sound profound by clothing it in technical language is pointless. It is also true that too many technical terms can hamper comprehension. We conclude, therefore, that the value of simple language depends on the nature of the subject and audience.

Projects

1. Select an informative discourse in Arnold, Ehninger, and Gerber's *The Speaker's Resource Book* (Scott, Foresman, 1966), and comment on the language. Was the speech intended for a popular audience? If so, is the language specific for that type of audience?
2. Find an article in a science magazine, such as *Scientific American* or *Natural History,* and write a paper on the ways in which language clarity has been achieved.
3. Select an article from a technical journal in your field of specialization. Do the requirements for accuracy, economy, and specificity differ from those of the speech in *The Speaker's Resource Book*? If so, in what way?
4. Give a speech in which you attempt to define an idea which is not immediately understandable. Write out this speech in manuscript form and read it. Give special attention to clarity of language.
5. Write a critical and descriptive statement about the language employed in a manuscript speech by one of your classmates.

20. Rudolph Flesch, "A New Readability Yardstick," *Journal of Applied Psychology,* June 1948, pp. 221-223. The most recent and widely used Flesch scales utilize only word length and sentence length, and exclude the Anglo-Saxon preference.

6.

FORMS OF CLARIFICATION

The main task of the informative speaker is to present his material so that the audience can comprehend it. As we have seen, clarity of language is one means of achieving this end. Proper selection of materials is another. In addition, clarification can be expedited by the use of (1) examples, (2) analogies, (3) history of discovery or development, and (4) visual aids. These forms may also be employed in persuasive discourse, but there the intent is different. The best example in the persuasive discourse is the one which best supports the case being made; the good example in the informative discourse is the one which makes clear the concept under consideration. Because the audience is predisposed to accept the informative communicator's word for it, he need not use examples to marshal his argument, but to shed light upon the subject. However, if the audience is in a mood to question his communication, then he must offer examples to support his case—hence he must turn to persuasion.

SELECTION OF MATERIALS

The one who knows a subject well (he is the one most likely to be invited to present informative speeches) must select the material which will best clarify a point for a particular audience. Anyone who has listened to those who convey information (for example, teachers) knows that some do a much better job than others in getting their material across. We have all heard such statements as, "Professor Geffert seems to know his subject, but I sure don't learn much from his lectures." The reasons are various. Professor Geffert may pay little attention to finding out about his audience and adapting to it. Perhaps his material is poorly organized, or he does not reinforce his ideas well. Perhaps he is verbose and has a monotonous delivery. Or perhaps he makes little use of the forms of clarification we shall discuss in this chapter. Effective clarification is that in which the communicator gives special attention to the forms that best convey his concepts in terms of the subject under discussion and the audience to which it is presented.

The task confronted by the informative communicator is to select from the available materials those which will make his subject clear to a specific audience. The classical term for the selective process is *invention,* and as conceived in the rhetorical tradition, it has to do with discovering what type of material is best for a specific communicative act. As Francis Bacon observed, "Invention is of two kinds, much differing; the one of Arts and Sciences, and the other, of speech and arguments."[1] In discussing the type of invention having to do with speech and arguments, he wrote,

> The invention of speech or argument is not properly an invention: for to invent is to discover that we know not, and not to recover or resummons . . . the scope and end of this invention is readiness and present use of our knowledge, and not addition or amplification thereof.[2]

The trap into which some speakers fall is to think that because they know a subject well, they have the necessary qualifications for conveying the material clearly to someone else. Of course, one *cannot* convey what he does not know, and to conclude otherwise is to court sophistry; but merely because one knows a subject well does not guarantee that he can inform others effectively. Many communicators without formal training in rhetoric do an excellent job of clarifying, but not without giving considerable thought to the means of presenting a particular subject so as to be better comprehended by a specific audience.

A statement by Ernst Cassirer in the introduction to his book *An Essay on Man* serves as an excellent point of departure for discussing the consideration the communicator must give to his vehicles of clarification:

1. Francis Bacon, *The Advancement of Learning* (New York: E. P. Dutton & Co., Inc., 1934), p. 290.
2. *Ibid.*, pp. 29 ff.

Of course it has not been possible to lay before their eyes the whole bulk of empirical evidence upon which my principal thesis rests. . . . I have had to content myself with citing those authors to whom I myself feel most indebted and with selecting those examples that seemed to me to be of typical significance and of paramount philosophical interest.[3]

Cassirer recognizes it as his rhetorical task to select material that will best get his point across to his readers: it is this task which confronts the informative communicator. One finds three principles of selection emerging from Cassirer's statement: (1) the material should faithfully reflect the speaker's point of view, (2) the examples should be typical for the subject matter, and (3) the material should be that most acceptable and appreciated by the audience.

Two speeches

In order to indicate the manner in which Cassirer's principles can be employed by a speaker as the basis for selecting material, let us examine two topics,—one in the humanities and the other in the sciences.

Let us suppose that one is giving a speech on "The Roles of the Suffering Servant in the Novels of William Faulkner." The speech is being given to a college speech class, most of whom have had courses in literature and have read one or two of Faulkner's novels. The speaker is an English major who has written a paper on the subject of his speech. He knows that he has more material than he can possibly present in six to eight minutes, and therefore he has the task of selecting that which will be the most helpful to the class. He also assumes that persuasion won't be necessary; the audience probably is not involved in any controversy concerning Faulkner and they consider the speaker an authority on the subject. Since the subject is literature, the speaker decides that the most effective means of clarification is to cite examples of suffering servants from Faulkner's novels. Since there are a number of examples, however, and time will permit only one or, at most, two, he has the task of selecting the character(s) who best exemplify the idea he is trying to illustrate. Cassirer's statement quoted above will be helpful in making this decision.

The speaker decides that the possible examples to use are Dilsey in *The Sound and the Fury*, Ruby Lamar in *Sanctuary*, Horace Benbow in *Sanctuary*, Nancy Mannigoe in *Requiem for a Nun*, Gavin

3. Ernst Cassirer, *An Essay on Man* (New Haven, Conn.: Yale University Press, 1944), p. viii.

Stevens in *Requiem for a Nun*, and Clytemnestra Sutpen in *Absalom, Absalom!* Cassirer's first principle is to *select the example which, in the speaker's opinion, best depicts his view*. In this case the speaker will select the character(s) who best depict what he means by the suffering servant. This may be done by the process of elimination; for instance, he decides to eliminate Ruby Lamar and Horace Benbow because they do not delineate the servant role as well as the others. Let us say that the speaker finally decides that the two most exemplary choices for the role as he understands it are Dilsey and Nancy. Cassirer's second criterion is to *select the examples which are most typical*. This criterion raises the question of which among the six seem to be most representative of Faulkner's characters in general. Dilsey, Nancy, Gavin, and Clytemnestra are all typical, but Dilsey and Nancy also have the advantage of better reflecting the author's point of view. Perhaps the most crucial task is the third — to *select the examples which are best known to the audience and likely to produce the most striking effect*. This can be accomplished by predicting what novels the students will most likely have read. Novels read in a required literature course or courses in American literature will serve as indicators. In most cases the novel which is best known is *The Sound and the Fury*. A motion picture based on the novel has appeared, and those who have not read the book may have seen the movie. In view of this consideration, Dilsey emerges as the best example. But the speaker is now confronted with a dilemma, inasmuch as he believes that Nancy, in *Requiem for a Nun*, best exemplifies his idea of the role of the suffering servant. He may decide, in view of the audience's knowledge, to discuss Dilsey first and then Nancy. If he does this, he will find it necessary to give more background information about Nancy than Dilsey. If the audience were one which had read a number of Faulkner's novels, the speaker could draw from any of the characters, but he would probably still use Nancy and Dilsey, since they seem most exemplary of the suffering servant. If time permitted, he could bring in more examples.

As a second case—one on a scientific subject—let us suppose that a speaker who has specialized in genetics wishes to explain genetic principles to a group of non-science majors. Perhaps this task also can best be achieved by the use of examples. First of all, following Cassirer's principles, the speaker will select examples from the types of life he knows best. If his major interest is botany, he will no doubt select plants; if zoology, animals. If he is an undergraduate, the examples he will know best are those employed in introductory genetics books—for instance, flower color in sweet peas, eye color in humans, human baldness, piebald coloring in human hair, and the fur color of guinea pigs. These are typical examples and thus fulfill the requirement of Cassirer's second criterion. We still must consider the third principle, however—that of finding material that will be acceptable to the particular audience. If the audience is composed of biology majors, classical examples from genetics such as the Drosophila (fruit flies) would probably be the best, since more experimental work has been done on the genetics of the Drosophila than on any other type of life. This would not be a good example for non-biology majors, however, since the genetic configurations of the Drosophila usually discussed are more complex than other forms.

Since the non-biology majors will require an elementary starting point, the best example will be the one which enables the speaker to start from the beginning and present the principles schematically. Examples such as color in sweet peas, horns in cattle, or eye color in humans all fulfill this requirement, so the author chooses his example on the basis of which one would most interest the particular audience. If most of the people in the audience are from a farm background, horns in cattle would be an excellent choice. If they are majors in horticulture or landscape architecture, sweet peas would be the best example. But most non-biology majors these days are from urban centers; in this case, human eye coloring is the best example. With this particular audience, if one wishes a second example to bring in additional principles (for example, sex-linked characteristics) or add freshness, since eye color is a common example, he could talk about human baldness. By carefully employing in this manner the criteria for selectivity proposed by Cassirer, the speaker maximizes the likelihood that audience understanding will be enhanced.

SPECIFIC MEANS OF PRESENTATION

The example

The contribution of the example to clarification is that it provides a specific point of contact between the subject matter and the audience. If the example is to serve this associative function well, it is crucial that the communicator select examples within the experience of the audience.

Examples are more powerful vehicles of clarification in some subjects than in others. A communicator clarifying principles in literary subjects is essentially limited to examples. If he wishes to discuss the poetic style of John Keats, he cannot very well achieve this end by the use of visual aids except by referring to the text which the listener has before him. Analogy or contrast may be helpful in comparing Keats with other poets, but the best means of clarification is to refer to the style of "Ode to Melancholy", "Ode to a Nightingale," or some other poem as an example. Other subjects in which examples are the most powerful form of clarification are psychology, sociology, economics, government, chemistry, and biology. In fact, the example is probably the most fruitful form of clarification for the most subjects. In subjects in which an object may be shown (such as botany and art) visual aids are more important; but visual aids are often employed as examples, and the criteria for their selection are the same. In some subject areas examples receive special designation. In psychology, an example is a *case study*, in philosophy, a *paradigm*. In art, examples are *representative paintings,* as also are *musical selections* which exemplify a composer's style. In chemistry or physics, the example may be an *experiment* conducted before the audience. In biology the *specimen* will often be an example. In archaeology or anthropology, the example may be an *artifact*, and in sociology examples may be *ideal types*.

There are two main kinds of examples. The first type, often employed in the sciences, is the *object* or *property*. The second type of example is the *concept*, used particularly in philosophy and theology. The function of an example which has to do with objects is to serve as a *representative type*. In the speech on genetics, eye color or baldness would have this purpose. In the sciences, the prerequisite for a good example is that it be representative and interesting to the audience. In contrast, in philosophy and theology, the example is often used as a *platform from which to build a point of view.* J. L. Austin uses "I name this ship the Queen Elizabeth" as an example of a performative utterance and from this he builds a theory about performative utterances.[4] In this case it is not crucial that the beginning point be representative of all performative utterances, though, of course, if some such utterances have other features, the other features will be of interest to the philosopher.

To clarify the nature of scientific examples, let us examine a speech in which a graduate student in meteorology talks to a graduate seminar composed of other students and professors. (We have already discussed the case in which a geneticist speaks to those who are uninformed. In this instance a specialist is speaking to other specialists.) The student's area of specialty is atmospheric electricity, and he decides to discuss the electrical currents in thunderstorms. In order to clarify the characteristics of such currents, he will select certain

---

4. J. L. Austin, *Philosophical Papers* (Oxford: Oxford University Press, 1961), pp. 222ff.

areas of thunderstorm activity as examples. First, he selects the area he knows the most about. If he has done his study in Florida, he will no doubt use this as the primary area about which to talk. However, electrical studies of thunderstorms are still in developmental stages and have been studied more in some regions than in others. These areas will be the ones reported in journal articles on the subject, and this will greatly influence the speaker's choice. In speaking to popular audiences, the example permitting the most schematic information is best; but when specialists speak to specialists, the example most widely cited by other specialists is the one which should be given preference. The final basis for selection is the type of specialization of the others in the seminar. If they are interested in climatology, synoptic meteorology, instrumental meteorology, or atmospheric acoustics, examples familiar to people in these specialties should be used if possible. In any case, the good scientific example is one which is representative; examples that have unusual features and do not clearly exhibit the point are of little help in clarifying an idea.

The example in philosophy or theology (and frequently in the theoretical sciences, such as physics) often is used to elaborate a conceptual model, or viewpoint. This is in contrast to the concrete scientific example, which usually exemplifies a principle. For example, if one wished to explain Boyle's law, he could briefly refer to helium and show how its behavior (under certain conditions of pressure and temperature) conforms to the law. The example in this case has rather rigid qualifications. A philosopher, in contrast, is not so rigidly bound in his examples (depending, of course, on his philosophical outlook). He may offer an example and proceed to build a whole philosophical system upon it. The example he selects will be less rigidly prescribed than that selected by the scientists, and will permit free movement in various directions. The main power of the philosopher's example is to provide a beginning point of common knowledge with the audience, so that they can move with him as he unfolds his point of view.

An excellent instance of such usage of the example may be found in Jean Paul Sartre's essay, "Existentialism Is a Humanism." Sartre addresses this essay to a popular audience rather than to specialists. In order to explain the concept of *abandonment*, Sartre gives the account of a student who, during the German occupation of France, came to him for advice. The student's mother and father quarreled frequently, and his father was inclined to be a collaborator. His elder brother had been killed in the German offensive of 1940, and he yearned to avenge him. He now lived alone with his mother; his problem was that he was sure his departure would cast her into despair, since she lived only for him. The decision he had to make was whether to stay with his mother or join the Free French forces. Even if he entered the forces, he might be assigned to paper work rather than the combat he so strongly desired. In this case, Sartre declares, regardless of what rules the boy might apply or whose advice he might seek, the choice still has to be his own. He is, therefore, abandoned to freedom and choice. "That is what 'abandonment' implies, that we ourselves decide our being." From this example, Sartre builds a view of the significance of choice if one is to exist as a man. The exactness of the example does not matter so much in this case as it would in science, since it is not the clearly defined nature of the example which gives it power, but the possibility for constructing from it a point of view. The example of Dilsey in the suffering-servant speech serves a similar function.

In a conceptual subject one example is enough, but in an exact discipline the communicator always fears that his example may not be representative. In exact subjects, statistics are sometimes preferred to examples, since they encompass more possibilities. But even the most exacting scientist employs examples in discourse, knowing their power of clarification. An authority in philosophy speaking to other philosophers will be more exact in his use of an example than when he speaks to a lay audience. But even when speaking to other philosophers, he uses his example for building his own theory and does not claim that it is typical of all the examples which are available to him.

Statistics

Statistics are discussed in this book under the rubric of example, inasmuch as they may be viewed as a certain kind or collection of examples put into mathematical form. Statistics accomplish four ends that are helpful for clarification: (1) counting, (2) measuring, (3) proportioning, and (4) comparing. Comparing is also a form of analogy, but we are concerned here with the statistical analogy only.

Statistics can do much to clarify certain points in exposition. To indicate that the University of Wisconsin has 34,000 students, that the Saturn Rocket is eighteen stories high, that 42 per cent of Americans are Catholic, or that Sirius is twenty-one times as luminous as the sun, can be of considerable help in clarifying a discussion of any of these topics. More complex statistics can be used with specialist audiences accustomed to thinking statistically (for example, a group of engineers hearing from a scientist how an atomic clock works). Statistics are most frequently employed in the sciences, social sciences, and psychology, but they also have their place in history and archaeology. Let us examine in detail some of the ways in which statistics may be helpful in clarification.

Counting. If one speaks about the Arab refugee problem in the Near East, the knowledge that the refugees number 230,000 would be useful. In talking about the New York University system, certain features are made clear if one is advised that it consists of forty-six colleges, thirty of them state-operated, and sixteen locally sponsored. If one is talking about Sinclair Lewis as an author, it would be helpful to know that he published ten novels.

Measuring. In giving a speech on bridges, one conveys some idea of size by stating that the Golden Gate Bridge is 4200 feet long, while the George Washington Bridge is 3500 feet. If one is talking about Canada, it is of some help to know that Canada consists of 3,851,809 square miles, of which 291,571 square miles are water. A speech about climbing the Matterhorn would be made more concrete by the information that the elevation of the mountain is 14,688 feet.

Proportioning. Proportioning is the statistics of percentages. When a speaker is discussing the population of Minnesota, it is significant knowledge that 7 per cent of the population is foreign-born and only 1 per cent nonwhite, and that of the foreign-born, about one half were born in Sweden, Norway, and Germany. In talking about government spending, the speaker can add clarity by pointing out that 50 per cent of all spending is on national defense.

Comparing. It is probably through comparison that statistics can be most helpful. A measurement or count is, in many cases, more decisive when compared with other statistics relating to items known by the audience. If one were speaking to a Pennsylvania audience about the city of Memphis, Tennessee, he could state that the population of Memphis (which is 497,524) is somewhat less than that of Pittsburgh (which is 604,322). In comparing the topography of the earth, a statement that Mt. Everest, which rises to 29,028 feet above sea level, would appear to scale on a globe with a diameter of 16 inches, only 0.012 inches high, is an excellent means of depicting irregularities in the earth's surface.

The reason that statistics are valuable as means of clarification is that they give the listener a sense of *size* and *proportion*. With these figures the auditor can compare counts, measurement, and proportions to those of objects with which he is already familiar. Sometimes the speaker may find it desirable to make such a comparison for the audience.

ANALOGY AND CONTRAST

A second significant means of clarifying ideas in discourse is through the use of analogy and contrast. By analogy and contrast I mean any type of comparison, regardless of whether it carries one into flights of fancy or relates two or more concrete, observable objects.

Literal vs. figurative

A traditional manner of classifying comparison is to distinguish between *literal* and *figurative analogies:* a literal analogy is usually said to be a comparison between two similar phenomena, while a figurative analogy is a comparison between two different orders of phenomena. This distinction is useful, since some analogies profess to be actual comparisons, while others are alike only in the imagination. For instance, in explaining the resistance of air pressure to the flight of a plane, a comparison could be made with waves that build up before the prow of a boat. This would be a literal comparison. But if the speaker stated that the resistance is similar to a huge hand coming down out of the sky and holding the plane back, the analogy would be figurative, since no one would suppose the hand were real.

A distinction between literal and figurative types of analogies is helpful when comparisons have to do with objects or properties of objects. If, however, a communicator intends to say something about the meaning of reality, the distinction between literal and figurative breaks down. Some kinds of reality cannot be depicted in literal or empirical language. In these cases, the speaker employs special types of analogies, such as *images, myths,* and *models.* Scientists and mathematicians sometimes employ models in order to work as precisely as possible with some concept or problem; but though they attempt to grasp a totality, they do not assume that the whole of reality has been contained within their model. Philosophers use myths in a similar manner. Plato in *The Republic*, in an attempt to express his view of reality, employed the myth of the cave. Now, of course, Plato did not intend to say we are actually in a cavern like the Mammoth Cave, but in another sense this is what he wished to express, for Plato's cave depicts what he sees as the human predicament of seeing only reflections, rather than reality itself.

Analogy of clarification vs. literary analogy

A further distinction in analogies is the difference between the *analogy of clarification* and the *literary analogy.* The literary analogy tries mainly to stir the imagination. In literature there is a distinction between the *metaphor* and the *simile*. The statement, "The Mackinac Bridge is an artery carrying the blood of life between Upper and Lower Michigan," is a metaphor. The information supplied by this sentence is limited, but the imagination is challenged. The analogy, "Life is like a sparrow which flits into the banquet hall at night, flies about for a time, only to return to the darkness of night," is a simile. More information may be conveyed here than in the previous example, since what can be stated about the whole of life in a sentence must be stated *analogically*. Nevertheless, the main intent of the simile is to portray an image, not to inform. The power of the literary analogy lies with the imagination and not with clarification. The focus of the analogy of clarification is to convey information.

At this point we might ask what makes analogies effective as avenues of clarification. Let us first consider the scientific analogy. In a scientific subject, the best analogy is the most exact one. The author, as a graduate student, heard a professor of speech science launch a fifteen-minute tirade against the analogy, often found in speech textbooks, that sound waves are similar to concentric circles moving out from a stone thrown into a lake. The professor rejected the analogy because of its inexactness; in the lake, waves are horizontal, whereas sound waves move from the mouth in all directions. In addition, the lake waves move out in a regular pattern, while the sound waves from the voice are directed in the area toward which the speaker is turned. Of the two analogies presented previously to depict pressure build-up in front of a plane's wing, the physicist would prefer the boat waves over the giant hand because it is more exact. Scientists often change basic analogies when they discover other, more exact ones. At one time geneticists thought that the beads on a string provided an excellent means of depicting the genes on a chromosome; but as electron microscopes came into use, geneticists discovered that some genes are spiral-thread-type structures in the chromosome, so the analogy of the spiral staircase is now more often employed because it is more exact. In the case of classical or Newtonian mechanics, the pendulum was used as an analogy from which to conceive laws in nature because of the regularity of the movement of the pendulum. But with the rise of quantum physics, the pendulum analogy had to be abandoned since nature, at least the movement of particles in atoms, was found to be irregular or indeterminate. The new analogy had to give some account of the irregularity of matter, and hence the model became a statistical one. Once again, the change was made in order to present an analogy which more exactly depicts the situation as the scientist sees it.

The scientific analogies discussed thus far have concerned general concepts. However, analogies which compare specific items are used more frequently by scientists. The clarifying power of the analogy lies in the ability to compare what the audience knows with what they have not yet grasped. Thus, the best analogy starts from what the audience knows and appreciates. A speaker, in discussing Russian history, may make a comparison between the freeing of the serfs in Russia in 1862 and the freeing of the slaves in the United States at about the same time. One can compare the features of Mars with those of the earth. In talking about penicillin mold, one can say it is similar to mold found on a spoiled orange. If a speaker is discussing the manner in which DNA controls the growth cycle in plants and animals, he can make a comparison with the computer which is programmed to feed information into an assembly arrangement, thereby manufacturing a product by automation. The computer analogy is being widely employed by biologists these days and is especially meaningful to those who are familiar with computer programs: experimental scientists, engineers, business accountants, and psychologists. The analogy will be less helpful to those in the humanities and arts, who thus far have made little use of computers.

The communicator often finds a clue to what sort of scientific analogies may be employed by examining the close relationship between analogy and discovery in science. Discovery in the sciences is often by analogy, as Morris Cohen points out. He discusses different sorts of scientific analogies and the manner in which they are used in discovery.[5] The planet Pluto was predicted by Lowell and Pickering before its actual discovery. The prediction was possible because of a comparison of the orbit of Neptune with other planetary orbits whose movement was affected by another planet. Some of the knowledge obtained in this way was not accurate, however. Clyde Tombaugh, who finally located the planet in 1930, found that Pluto was neither as large nor as bright as predicted. Nevertheless, the means of discovery was through analogy with what was known about other planets. If one wished to talk about the orbits of planets, he might find the analogy through which Pluto was discovered a useful means of explaining the concept. Even more suggestive, perhaps, is the analogy of the manner in which DNA controls life. The computer analogy used in this case has helped conceptualize the discovery, and it is this same analogy that the biologist employs as he goes on to make new discoveries. In the search for an analogy through which to clarify a complex idea a speaker should always determine if he can use some analogy that was employed in the discovery of the idea.

The analogy is particularly helpful when a communicator wishes to explain a complex idea to an uninformed audience. In 1940, when

5. Morris R. Cohen and Ernest Nagel, *An Introduction to Logic and Scientific Method* (New York: Harcourt, Brace & World, Inc., 1934), pp. 221ff.

the atomic nature of matter was little understood by anyone without a college education, Henry Schacht employed an effective analogy which enabled almost anyone to grasp the idea. He observed that if one were to stand on a handkerchief and begin shrinking, he would notice the structures of the fabric. When he had shrunk enough, he would even be able to observe the atomic structure of the carbon atoms in the cotton.[6] The power of this analogy is its ability to help the listener gain a perspective of the size of the atom and its relation to other structures of the materials, such as fibers and molecules.

When specialists communicate with other specialists, however, analogies for clarification are not of such consequence, though some may be used. Specialists know many of the concepts and specifics from first-hand experience and can make their own comparisons without the communicator doing it for them. When comparisons are made in scientific papers, great care must be taken to assure exactness; the scientific audience will not appreciate loose or inaccurate analogies.

The analogy in theoretical subjects

Finally, we need to notice the characteristics of the analogy in theoretical subjects, such as philosophy, theology, and physics. If one assumes (as did the logical positivists of the Vienna Circle) that philosophy should be concerned with sense verification, philosophical analogies are exactly like those of the sciences. However, theoretical concepts call for analogies of a different order. Analogies in these disciplines serve as a starting place from which to develop a point of view. (The analogy of science, in contrast, is concerned with discovery, hence exactness refined by sense data.) A system or model is not, in the final analysis, a discovery. No one insists, for example, that Hegel *discovered* his dialectical philosophy. Neither do scientists, who these days admit the value of models, claim that their models are discoveries about the world, even though they assume that in some measure their models explain what goes on in the world.

The theoretical aspects of science, especially physics, in which systems models are important, employ analogies similar to those in the humanities, though they require more empirical rigor than do the analogies in the humanities. Certain philosophies, on the other hand, use analogies that are much more open-ended. Two examples, the first from philosophy and the second from physics, will serve to clarify this point.

Søren Kierkegaard in his *Philosophical Fragments* employs an analogy which becomes crucial for his theology of revelation and

6. Henry Schacht, "Touring the Atomic World," *California Monthly*, May 1940.

incarnation. He tells the story of a prince who was once riding through the realm when he chanced upon a peasant maiden with whom he fell in love. He decided to marry her, but he wanted her to love him for himself. He knew that awed by his princely position, she would not refuse. If she did reject him, he could win her by presenting her with magnificent gifts, but by doing so he would win her by his magnificence rather than for himself. After considering the dilemma for some time, the prince put on the clothes of a peasant and went to live in her village. In this way, he would know that if he won her, it would be because she loved him for himself. It is in the same manner, so Kierkegaard affirms, that God, in Jesus Christ, seeks out man's love. From Kierkegaard's analogy a whole theology can be unfolded.

In physics, an analogy of a similar nature attempts to express the second law of thermodynamics, a law which is fundamental to the theoretical basis of information theory:

> The famous second law of thermodynamics states that in an isolated system, entropy may stay constant or increase, but never decrease. For an analogy, consider a shoebox into which one puts a handful of white beads at one end and a handful of black beads at the other. If the box is never touched, the beads will stay in their respective ends, i.e., entropy (disorder) will stay constant. However, the moment the box is disturbed the beads will begin to mix, and disorder, i.e., entropy will increase.[7]

From this analogy one can construct a system with which to examine numerous communication events. The analogy meets the exact demands made upon such a comparison in the sciences which were not made in the case of the analogy which Kierkegaard employed.

Of course, analogies concerned with more restricted matters do appear in philosophy and theology. One may compare and contrast Kant's idea of the transcendental ego with that of Edmund Husserl or Jean Paul Sartre, or one may compare Friedrich Schleiermacher's religious feeling with Jonathan Edwards' religious affection. One may also compare the novel technique of Turgenev with that of Hemingway, or the painting of Cézanne with that of Picasso.

The contrast

The contrast may be of more help in some cases than the comparison. Contrasts are not employed in order to set forth a philosophy,

7. Francis Bellow, *Readings in Communication from Fortune*, ed., Francis William Weeks (New York: Holt, Rinehart & Winston, Inc., 1961), p. 7.

model, or system, but they are good for highlighting specific differences. The requirement of a good contrast is that it bring into sharp focus the view to be clarified. The most helpful contrast is one in which the view from which the contrast originates is known by the listeners, but contrasts can often be effective without this prior audience knowledge. Suppose, for instance, that one wished to explain the existentialist view of ambiguity of language. This might best be explained by contrast with a different view held by the general semanticists. The contrast is useful even though the auditors might not be acquainted with the general semanticist view.

The general semanticist assumes that words are ambiguous in proportion to their level of abstraction from sense-perceived objects and experiences. The least ambiguous word, therefore, is the word which points to specific objects. When one moves from words referring to objects to generalizations about these objects, he is moving to a higher level of abstraction. Abstractions can proliferate, so that ideas become more and more abstract. The more abstract words become, so the general semanticist declares, the more ambiguous they are likely to be. He therefore insists that in order to clear up ambiguities, one must move back down the levels of abstraction until he reaches a level which may be shared by the auditor. For the existentialist, in contrast, the ambiguity of words is the result of different ways in which individuals and groups perceive the world. Each individual, if he exists authentically, chooses his world. Language is, of course, public, but because A's world is different from B's as the result of the choices he has made, what A means by the word *alienation* may differ considerably from what B means. Ambiguity is therefore overcome only as A exposes his inner affirmations to B (Sartre), or inasmuch as both participate in transcendence (Jaspers), or inasmuch as grace provides communion (Kierkegaard). By this contrast, the concepts of the existentialist concerning ambiguity become more clear, and are set forth in bold relief. This contrast, of course, has greater force and interest value if the audience knows about general semantics, but it still clarifies to a considerable extent even for those who do not.

The difference between humanistic analogies for specialized groups as compared with popular audiences must also be noted. In the humanities, specialists, in talking to other specialists, do less informing and more arguing than in some sciences. Analogies, when employed, thus are introduced largely for the purpose of argument. Informing in the humanities therefore serves only a genetic function, i.e., providing the novice with enough background insight so that he is able to enter the arena of argument.

Relating the history of discovery or development can be a method of structure rather than a type of clarification, since it involves a time sequence. But used as a method of clarification it is different enough from other methods to warrant special consideration. The main purpose of a chronological structure is to give unity to a discourse. The history of development or discovery as clarification, on the other hand, unfolds complex ideas in such a way that what is simpler precedes or, in other cases, is contrasted with that which is more complex. The contrast is not always from the simple to the more complex, since what is prior in time might actually be more intricate, but the comparison should nevertheless serve to make the new concept clearer. In understanding an idea, some understanding of the situation and presuppositions out of which the idea grew can be helpful. Even in science, systems and theories admittedly contain presuppositions. When these systems are set forth in their historical development, the presuppositions upon which they rest become obvious. Francis Bacon argued that science could best advance by disclosing its presuppositions.

> He who would promote the growth of the sciences should be less solicitous about the trunk or body of them, and bend his care to preserve the roots and draw them out with some little earth about them.[8]

Furthermore, an approach which discloses presuppositions treats auditors as persons rather than as mere recording devices for cataloguing results or conclusions. Plato would agree, for he felt it important that one know not only the right conclusion, but the reason for it. When specialists speak to other specialists they normally reveal their presuppositions, thus treating their auditors as persons. Unfortunately, however, in communication with popular audiences, the methods and presuppositions are often eliminated and only conclusions reported. The value of presenting a complex idea through noting its history of discovery or development is that ideas or discoveries are usually worked out against a prior or differing belief. By presenting the thought processes through which the discoverer or developer went, we can focus more sharply on the idea being clarified. In this way it becomes obvious what he is denying and what he is affirming when he offers a new idea. By learning how Heisenberg developed his indeterminancy principle against a background of

8. Francis Bacon, *Advancement of Learning* (New York: E. P. Dutton & Co., Inc., 1934), VI, 2.

Newtonian mechanics, we learn Heisenberg's presuppositions and see his principle in bolder relief.

In order to indicate the manner in which the history of development or discovery may be helpful in clarifying a complex idea, we shall explore three examples. The first has to do with atomic theory, the second with Freud's dream theory, and the third with Charles Peirce's pragmatism.

(1) *Atomic Theory.* The man to whom the atomic theory of nature is attributed is John Dalton (1766–1844). The Greeks—Democritus, Leucippus, and, later, Epicurus—had presented an atomic theory, but during the Middle Ages their views were largely ignored. In the sixteenth and seventeenth centuries, support for the atomic theory of matter was given by such men as Francis Bacon, René Descartes, and Isaac Newton. It was Dalton, however, who first presented a detailed atomic theory. In Dalton's time the favorite manner of accounting for compounds was the *phlogiston theory.* Phlogiston was considered a fundamental element (for example, George Ernst Stahl said fire) which became a compound when combined with some substance. Even when oxygen was discovered and shown to make water when combined with hydrogen, some chemists (Joseph Priestley, for example) refused to abandon the idea that compounds are created by the combination of phlogiston and some other substance. Dalton offered a view which not only differed from the phlogiston explanation but which was built on the old Greek atomic view of nature. He suggested that compounds are made up of a number of elements with different sorts of atoms and that even though the weights of these atoms differ they combine to form a compound. By experimentation, scientists discovered that Dalton's view offered a much better explanation than the phlogiston theory of what happened in the formation of compounds.

Other details could be added to the ones presented, but this account is sufficient to show the manner in which a history of development helps clarify an idea. Because the presuppositions are brought out in the open, a more penetrating insight is attained than if the speaker merely informed his audience that all matter consists of atoms of different weights, and that they combine to form the compounds which we observe in nature, such as water and salt.

(2) *Freud's Dream Theory.* Before Freud, dreams were often looked upon as predictions of events about to occur, or perhaps as an expression of anxieties. Freud offered the new view that dreams are primarily forms of wish fulfilment. That which a person dreams is often what he wishes were so, or fears might be so. But the manner in which dreams reveal wishes cannot be seen simply and superficially. Freud's dream interpretation has to be seen in the light of his

division of the mind into the *conscious* and the *unconscious*. It was in his affirmation of the unconscious that Freud differed from his contemporaries. A subconscious region of the mind had been previously suggested, but not seriously explored. As Freud constructed his theory of the mind, he decided that dreams which involve such objects as snakes, cathedrals, or cards, must be interpreted as wishes of the subconscious mind. Once this was decided, the next question was what these symbols, as Freud called them, meant. Since Freud believed sex to be a fundamental human desire, he gave each of the symbols an interpretation in which sex was involved in one way or another. These desires, he argued, are not openly manifest, but are repressed in the subconscious; for that reason, dreams are crucial for discovering what is in the subconscious mind. Freud believed that dreams are a valuable tool in psychoanalysis because they provide additional data from which to determine the nature of neuroses. By discussing the significance of dreams in this way, Freud's presuppositions are disclosed and one has a much better comprehension of his dream interpretation than if the communicator had merely explained the interpretation of the symbols.

(3) *Charles Peirce's Pragmatism.* In order to explain a philosophical position, it is often extremely valuable to proceed by a history of development, inasmuch as most philosophy is worked out as a reaction against another philosophy. Charles Peirce, the "father of pragmatism," presented his views as a reaction against the "clear and distinct ideas" of Descartes. Peirce pointed out that Descartes hoped to make ideas clear by employing words exactly through the use of definitions. Peirce agreed with Descartes that familiarity is the first step toward clearness, and the defining of terms the second. He charged, however, that nothing new can be learned merely by analyzing definitions. Peirce offered as a substitute his famous principle, "Consider what effects, that might conceivably have practical bearings, we conceive the object of our conception to have. Then, our conception of these effects is the whole of our conception of the object." From this premise he proceeded to argue that ideas become clear and distinct, not by offering definitions, but by raising the question of what practical effects the concept might have. It is by the practical effects that the "trueness" of a concept is to be determined — hence its clarity. Clearness therefore requires observation and experimentation rather than mere cogitation, as Descartes would have it. In this manner Peirce rejected Cartesian dualism, which separates the subject from the object.

Peirce's views are related to English empirical realism, but instead of limiting "truth" to ideas which arise from sense experience, he was willing to commence with ideas of any kind. If an idea is to be given any credence, however, its practical effects must be shown; or, in other words, verification is through experience. By indicating the manner in which Peirce worked out his views against the backdrop of modern philosophy, one has a clearer perception of his ideas. History of discovery or development may be of more help to the popular audience than to an audience of specialists, inasmuch as the specialist often already knows background of this sort. But in case he does not, this method of clarification is of help even to him.

VISUAL AND AURAL AIDS

Two final forms of clarification, and significant ones for many subjects, are visual and aural aids. These forms of clarification are crucial because they bring added dimensions of perception to the subject matter at hand. A girl in one of my classes wished to talk about the coati-mundi, a South and Central American raccoon-like animal, about which she had considerable knowledge because her family had raised a number of them as pets. Had she in the speech compared the coati to the raccoon, she would have helped us in knowing what the animal was like. Had she brought pictures, it would have helped more. She could have pointed out the raccoon features of the tail and feet, but the flexible snout which is unlike that of the raccoon. But what she did was even more effective: she brought her coati-mundi and pointed out the features of the pet as she talked. The actual bending of the snout before the class was much more memorable than a picture of the snout could ever be. The visual presence of the coati produced such a striking effect that I remember most of the details of the speech, even though it was given several years ago.

Visual aids are particularly valuable in the sciences. In biology, a subject in which life processes of animals and plants are discussed, such aids are indispensable. In addition to the visual aids employed in the lectures, students are sent to laboratories for further viewing of specimens and life processes as seen under the microscope. Visual aids are also of great use in the physical sciences (although less so as one approaches the theoretical aspects of physics). In engineering and the graphic arts visual aids are crucial. In comparing styles of architecture or painting, if a speaker does not employ pictures in some form or another he will be almost totally ineffective. A speech comparing Byzantine and Gothic architecture needs pictures and models so that the distinctive features of each can be pointed out. Subjects in which numerous statistics and mathematical comparisons are employed also need visual representation. We all have had the experience of hearing a speaker present a series of statistics which we could not begin to remember or even comprehend. However, when such figures are presented by the use of visual aids, we often find the statistics very helpful.

Aural aids are likewise indispensable to topics where sound is involved. A student in one of my classes compared the traditional eight-note musical scale with a five-note scale. He used visual aids to make the comparison, writing the musical notations on the board. The comparison was effective from the standpoint of music theory, but most of us in the class had never to our knowledge heard music in which a five-note scale was used. Thus, in spite of our understanding of the theory of the five-note scale, we could not form an aural image and therefore probably could not identify such music were we to hear it. Leonard Bernstein has lectured very effectively on both jazz and classical music by talking about a musical form and then playing representative scores (sometimes on the piano, but often with the orchestra) to illustrate his point.[9] Although aural aids are extremely useful in some situations, visual aids are used more commonly, and the rest of our discussion will concentrate on them.

Visual and aural aids do have limitations. The old adage, "A picture is worth a thousand words," is true only if the concept that one wishes to describe can be pictured graphically. Speeches having to do with objects, either natural or created, lend themselves well to the use of visual aids. However, in the humanities, where many concepts are verbal in nature, the visual or aural aids are not very useful. If one wishes to explain *dialectical materialism*, which is the philosophical underpinning of Marxism, one might get some assistance from visualization by showing the triadic relationship thus:

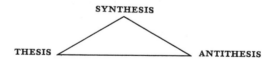

But even so, the verbal explanation would be more conducive to comprehension than the visual aid. If one wishes to explain the *stream-of-consciousness technique* in literature, it is difficult to design visual aids which are of help, and the same is true if a speaker wishes to talk about *existentialism, neo-orthodoxy, neo-classicism,* or *neo-Thomism*. In these subjects, clarification must proceed by analogies and examples.

However, aids are not employed solely to indicate specific objects;

9. Bernstein's speech on jazz may be found in Carroll Arnold, Douglas Ehninger, and John Gerber, *The Speaker's Resource Book* (Glenview, Ill.: Scott, Foresman and Company, 1966), pp. 67–77.

they may also be used to convey totalities. Even when *pictures* do not help, an *outline* of the ideas to be covered may assist the audience in seeing the subject in its total perspective. For instance, if one is giving a speech on Plato's *Symposium*, he will wish to point out that the book consists of speeches. It will help the audience both in keeping track of the speakers and in grasping the names if the speaker puts them in order on the blackboard or chart, or projects them via slide or opaque projector:

1. Phaedrus
2. Pausanias
3. Eryximachus
4. Aristophanes
5. Agathon
6. Socrates
7. Alcibiades

In this manner, the total number of speakers can be visualized as well as their time order in relation to each other.

Or, if one is presenting Thomas Aquinas' five proofs for the existence of God, one could list them on the blackboard or chart so that the order and interrelationships could be seen in total perspective:

1. The argument from motion
2. The argument from the nature of efficient cause
3. The argument from possibility and necessity
4. The argument from the gradation of things
5. The argument concerning ends

In case a listener wants to set straight in his own mind how the fifth way differs from the first, he can easily recall the first by glancing at the chart.

A chart identifying the various positions in a governmental division is also useful to an audience in grasping the total structure and the relations of the divisions to each other, and in keeping the component parts separated. The structure of the federal reserve system may be diagramed as shown on page 92. In this case, the chart not only contains the major divisions, but includes other detailed information which gives the listener perspective as to size. In this way the vital statistics may also be visualized.

Visual aids are numerous in form. Those commonly employed are blackboards and flannel boards, actual objects (such as a scubadiving suit), speaker-prepared charts on poster cardboard or other material, commercially prepared charts (such as a chemical element chart); maps (both student- and commercially drawn), pictures, models (for example, one of a larynx), and various projection-type aids such as slides, film strips, opaque projectors, and movies.

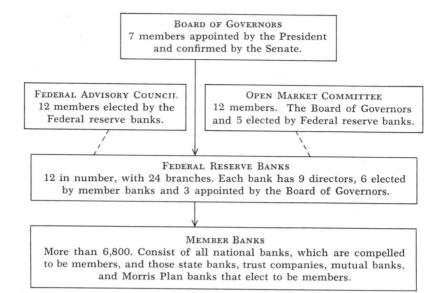

The mechanics of visual aids

In order to indicate the ways in which visual aids should be prepared and presented, two examples are provided here, the first having to do with a speech about the human ear, and the second a speech about communication in which a communication model is presented.

The human ear. In preparing a speech the first step is to plan the speech and then to determine places at which visual aids will assist in conveying the necessary material. It is only in a speech class that a speaker might have the luxury of selecting a visual aid and then forming a speech around it. In almost all other situations the information to be conveyed is the first consideration, and the preparing or securing of visual aids follows.

In a speech on the human ear the speaker will first want to give the audience an overall view of the structures of the ear. In order to do so he will prepare a diagram which presents the gross structures (see opposite page). In this diagram only the gross structures are shown. The reason is that it is important for the audience to identify the main parts of the ear before details are noted. At this stage, more detail would only confuse the listener. This is why it is better for the speaker to prepare his own charts unless commercial ones with varying degrees of detail are available. A chart which presents all the detailed structures of the ear will take the listener's attention away

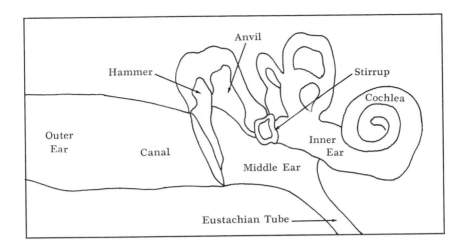

from the main outline of the outer, middle, and inner ear. Instead of drawing the representation it is usually possible to find pictures in books and pass the pictures around; speakers often do this, but the method is very unsatisfactory. First of all, the speaker cannot point out what needs to be seen by the auditor as the picture moves from person to person. Secondly, the speaker must continue with his presentation, and as each person takes up the book his attention is called away from what the speaker is then saying. A safe rule is that a speaker should never pass out anything to an audience unless he has enough copies available for each person in the audience. If one mimeographed the above diagram of the ear so that a copy would be available for each person in the audience, the speaker could point out a structure and each person could see it on his own sheet. If the speaker constructs only one diagram on posterboard he needs to be certain that the diagram can be seen by everyone in the room; thus the size will be determined by how large the room is. Once I heard a speech in which the speaker used a large chart to display the statistics of a college fund-raising drive. Rather than reading the figures, he pointed to them and went on to the next part of the speech. This was an excellent use of visual aids, the only difficulty being that the auditorium was large and only those in the front half could read the chart. Before long those in the back commenced whispering or reading. Thus an effective speaking technique ended in disaster because the visual aid was too small.

To return to our speech on the human ear, when the overall structure of the ear has been presented the speaker will want to prepare at least two additional diagrams which are more detailed — one of the middle ear and another of the inner ear. For the inner ear he may require a second diagram showing the receptive nerves in detail and a third showing the internal distribution of the nerves. A diagram of the receptive nerves in the cochlea is shown here:

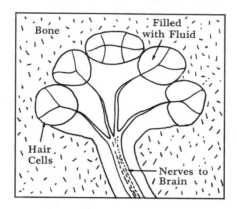

Because of the detail of these drawings it is necessary to prepare them before the speech. If one attempts to do this while he is talking, he will have to pause, and will hence lose his audience, unless he is talented at talking and drawing at the same time. If the situation permits, one might draw the diagrams on the blackboard before the speech, but this is not the most effective way because the audience will miss the early part of the speech because they will be looking at the various diagrams.

Once the speaker has outlined his material and prepared his visual aids, he is ready to give his speech. But the effective presentation of visual aids also requires planning ahead. It is necessary for the speaker to be familiar with the setting in which he is to give his speech in order to know where he will put his visual aids and the manner in which they will be held in place. Visual aids are the most effective if they are brought out at the time the speaker is ready to refer to them. The three or four ear diagrams should not be displayed so that they can be examined at the beginning of the speech. Rather, each should be presented at the appropriate time. If this is done, arrangements need to be made so that they can be placed where they may be seen. Unless hooks or some other arrangements are available, the best method is to attach masking tape to the drawing before beginning the speech. It is important to use masking tape because it is much easier to work with than cellophane tape and one does not have to worry about inadvertently removing paint when the chart is taken down. Charts drawn or mounted on posterboard will seldom stand by themselves, and many a visual aid has been ineffective because the speaker did not prepare a method for supporting his chart.

As to placing the charts, they must be located so that they can be seen over the heads of those in the front row. Normally it is better to locate visual aids in the middle of the room so the speaker can stand either to the left or right of the aids and face the audience. If the speaker points with the right hand he should stand so that the chart is on his right when he faces the audience. The reverse is the case if he points with his left hand. The reason for this position is that it permits the greatest ease in pointing at the object and looking at the audience simultaneously. The speaker should always remember that he should speak to the audience and not to the visual aid. Pointing is essential in using visual aids because if the aid is to be of help the auditor needs to be shown specifically what the speaker is talking about. In showing the location of the hair cells in the cochlea, the speaker should point directly to the points where they are found rather than motioning in the general direction of the receptive nerve diagram.

Communication model

Let us suppose that a speaker were going to use the blackboard to show a communication model in a speech on communication. Before starting the speech he would draw the model on the board thus:

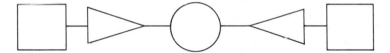

He should make sure the model is high enough and large enough to be seen by everyone in the audience and near the center of the room so he can work with it easily. After some introductory statements he refers to the model, (in this case, an electrical transmission). As he takes up the five components of the diagram he writes the word "source" above the first symbol, discusses it, then moves on to the next and writes "encoder" above it. When he has finished this stage of the speech his model will look like this:

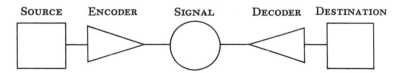

Now his task is to apply concretely to the speaking situation the components which are labeled with the vocabulary of electrical transmission. As he discusses each he will write under the symbols the following:

Intentive behavior of the speaker	Encoding behavior of the speaker	Message	Decoding behavior of the hearer	Interpretative behavior of the hearer

While he is writing these words he should look at his audience as much as possible, but this will require practice. Effectively used visual aids usually require practice in their use prior to giving the speech. If one does not plan the use of his visual aids they will tend to use him—that is, get in his way. Visual aids, if used poorly, can even detract from an otherwise effective speech.

The modes of clarification discussed in this chapter can do much to help clarify complex concepts. Discretion must be used by the speaker so as to employ those modes which are best suited to the subject and audience.

Projects

1. Read an informative discourse and notice the modes of clarification that are employed. Suggest ways in which additional modes of clarification may have improved the discourse. Did you notice any means of clarification not discussed in this chapter?
2. In the reading you are doing for other classes, see if you can locate the use of history of development or discovery. Does this approach help you to better understand the concept presented? Why?
3. Can the same example be employed in two different speeches, one of which is informative and the other persuasive? Can you account for any differences between the two usages?
4. Evaluate the modes of clarification employed by one of your classmates in his speech. Can you suggest additional ways in which he could have clarified his material which would have made his communication more effective?
5. Which one of your professors do you consider the most effective as a lecturer? To what do you attribute his effectiveness? Do his modes of clarification play a significant role?
6. What mode or modes of clarification are employed chiefly in the communication of the profession you expect to enter?
7. Select a professor who employs visual aids effectively. How do you account for the effectiveness of their use?

7.

REINFORCING

AND EMPHASIZING

We have located informative communication as occurring in the situation in which someone who knows conveys his knowledge to someone who does not. When the audience is thus unfamiliar with the content of the speech, they are likely to have some difficulty in comprehension, and reinforcement and emphasis of ideas will be needed. The problem exists both in speaking and in writing, but it is more acute with oral communication. Written material profits through reinforcement, but in spoken discourse, reinforcement is crucial. The reader can always go back over material which is difficult, but the listener is normally unable to do so. The nature of reinforcement in speech differs, depending on whether the communicator is presenting all his material in one discourse, or in a series of lectures or articles. In this book the main concern is the informative discourse which must be completed on a single occasion.

REINFORCEMENT

The word *reinforcement* has two very different meanings as applied to informative speaking and writing. The older, more widely known meaning has much in common with the way the term is used in both building construction and military terminology: in this sense, "to reinforce" is to add something that will bolster, strengthen, or support a point. In the case of informative speaking, this can refer to ways of making some concept or unit of information more striking, salient, or memorable. In recent years, however, "reinforcement" has been used as a technical term in psychology, where it refers to reward and punishment techniques for establishing certain kinds of learned behavior in men and animals. One way of maintaining the distinction between these two meanings of the term is to remember that in the older, more common sense, what one "reinforces" is a point in the speech; whereas in the newer, specialized psychological meaning, one "reinforces" the listener. We shall see that both meanings of the term apply to informative speaking.

Psychological research in reinforcement is done primarily by those who conceive of learning in terms of behavior. In everyday terms, any means of positive reinforcement may be considered a "reward" for "proper" behavior.[1] Some learning seems to grow out of such reinforcement—for example, learning passageways through mazes or memorizing a series of nonsense syllables or numbers. For learning systems, models, or ultimate notions, however, most learning does not seem to be of this sort. Here learning is by insightful comprehension. It is difficult to know how such concepts as Freud's dream theory, quantum mechanics, stream of consciousness, or Cézanne's theory of central focus in painting could be taught by laying behavior upon behavior, or concept upon concept. The behavioral approach is atomistic, whereas these cases require that the learner grasp a total configuration. It is precisely because man constructs systems, models, and ultimate notions (while animals do not) that results drawn from experiments with animal learning have only limited application to the learning of complex concepts.

Reinforcement theory best explains how one learns a foreign language, memorizes formulae in organic chemistry, or masters other rote behaviors. Programmed learning, which is based on reinforcement theory, has been most successful when applied to teaching such subjects. Previously we have noted that informative speaking is concerned more with complex concepts than with rote behaviors; but it is important to remember that *listening is behavior*, and for that reason psychological reinforcement theory applies in certain ways to informative speaking.

For example, effective informative discourse requires that the audience be continuously motivated to listen. Motivation is most powerful when it results from the individual's expectation of satisfying some need or desire; and the speaker who provides many such satisfactions during the speech keeps his audience motivated to continue listening. It is for this reason that a speaker so often finds it easy to talk to an audience who obviously desire the information he has to give them. As each bit of information is presented, it both

1. C. Ferster and B. F. Skinner, *Schedules of Reinforcement* (New York: Appleton-Century-Crofts, 1957). G. A. Kimble, *Hilgard and Marquis' Conditioning and Learning* (New York: Appleton-Century-Crofts, 1961).

satisfies an existing desire and generates the expectation that further satisfactions will follow if listening is continued.

The audience with little interest at the beginning of the speech may be elevated to a higher level of motivation by explaining the significance of the subject to them (which is another way of saying that the speaker explains why the listeners need the information or should desire it). Two further ways of motivating an audience to listen are by the use of *humor* and *internal summaries.*

Some informative speakers use humor at the beginning of the speech and at the end of each major idea. The audience soon learns that a joke will be the reward for struggling through a difficult concept. It is important to remember, however, that this technique works only if the humor is intrinsic — that is, only if it depends for its effect upon a grasp of the ideas in the preceding portion of the speech. If the humor is extrinsic — that is, if it consists of stories that would be just as funny if they were told by themselves — the listener will not have to attend to the speaker's main points at all, but can obtain his "reward" simply by listening for the cues that tell him a point has ended and a joke has begun. Because such reinforcement is not contingent upon listening to the ideas in the speech, it does very little to reinforce good listening behavior. By the use of extrinsic humor the speaker may do much to enhance his reputation as a raconteur, but he is not making his humor serve the informative purpose of the speech.

A second way of reinforcing the act of listening is by the use of internal summaries and other devices that tell listeners that some portion of the informative task has been completed. Most people are reinforced by any sense of concrete accomplishment — by an awareness that they have finished some task or some significant part of a task. If the speaker lays out at the beginning of the speech the exact ground he intends to cover, then periodically reminds the audience that certain significant segments have been dealt with, he provides his listeners with a continuing sense of achievement throughout the speech; and this sense of achievement will often enhance the motivation to listen.

EMPHASIS

We have just seen how reinforcement in the psychological sense applies to informative speaking. In the older sense (as a technique for strengthening or bolstering particular points in the speech), reinforcement is often equated with *emphasis.* Effective informative discourse highlights the most important concepts so that they get greater attention from the audience.

Raymond Ehrensberger, in a classical study, discovered that the most effective means of emphasizing an idea is to call attention to it by such language as "Now get this."[2] He also discovered that changing the rate of delivery and pausing and gesturing gave emphasis and thus enhanced effectiveness. Another means of emphasis sometimes proposed is raising or lowering the volume of the voice, but Ehrensberger did not find these differences in vocal force as significant a means of emphasis. The results of Ehrensberger's study were as follows:

RANK	DEVICE	EXPERI- MENTAL MODE % OF RIGHT ANSWERS	NEUTRAL MODE % OF RIGHT ANSWERS	STATISTICAL ANALYSIS
1	"Now get this" (Verbal emphasis)	86	53.2	Very significant difference
2	Three distributed repetitions	78	51.4	Very significant difference
3	Repeat (early in speech)	72	50.7	Very significant difference
4	Slow	76	59.8	Very significant difference
5	Repeat (late in speech)	67	50.7	Very significant difference
6	Pause	69	55.4	Very significant difference
7	Gesture	66	53.2	Very significant difference
8	Four distributed repetitions	60	51.4	Significant difference
9	Two distributed repetitions	58	51.4	No real difference
10	Soft voice	56	55.4	No real difference
11	Loud voice	51	59.8	Significant negative difference

2. Raymond Ehrensberger, "Experimental Study of the Relative Effectiveness of Certain Forms of Emphasis in Public Speaking," *Speech Monographs*, XII:2 (1945), 94–111.

This study was carried out using a control group to which a speech with neutral emphasis and repetitions was given. The same speech was given to other groups with the devices listed above. Following the speech all the students were given a test on the content; the percentage of right answers was as reported above.

REPETITION

A significant means of calling attention to important ideas is the use of repetition, as can be noted in Ehrensberger's results. From this table it is evident that repetitions have a decided effect on retention until after four repetitions; then the effect diminishes. As few as two distributed repetitions, however, apparently create no real change. We cannot be sure that these statistics would be the same if the students tested were on a higher level, or were people from other facets of society. Experimentation by Thistlewaite, de Haan, and Kamenetsky indicates that the more intelligent an audience, the less obvious a point needs to be in order that it be grasped.[3] Another complicating factor might be that repetition is more effective with auditors who know only a little about a topic than with those who are somewhat knowledgeable. Nevertheless, some benefit seems to result in any case.

The type of repetition employed will vary according to whether the material has to do with performance or with conceptualization. In the case of performance, repetition involves repeating what is to be done in a schematic way so that the main steps are clear. When one explains the construction of a computer program, repeating the steps covered at certain stages will be of help because so many steps are involved. At the conclusion of the speech it would be well for the speaker to include a summary, recalling the major steps in the process. The same type of repetition would help in a speech about the use of a university placement service. The steps in applying and interviewing for a position are so numerous that some repetition would make memorization easier. A well-prepared speech may not normally need a summary, but if a process involves a number of steps, a well-constructed summary may enhance learning considerably.

In subjects which concern complex concepts rather than performance, effective repetition is achieved by saying the same thing in a different manner. This repeating in a different way is particularly helpful in conveying the complex ideas of such subjects as physics,

3. D. L. Thistlewaite, H. de Haan, and J. Kamenetsky, "The Effects of 'Directive' and 'Non-directive' Communication Procedure on Attitudes," *Journal of Abnormal Social Psychology*, LI (1955), 107–113.

philosophy, and theology. If one wishes to explain the second law of thermodynamics, he can begin with the observation that heat will not flow from one body to another at a higher temperature than it entered the first. Another way of repeating this explanation would be by the use of an analogy. The analogy presented by Bellow of black and white marbles in a box (see page 84) is such a means. The marbles in the box never become more ordered regardless of how long they are shaken, just as the heat which departs never increases as it gets farther from the source. Still another manner of repetition is by the use of an example. In my basement is a gas hot water furnace. The gas in burning heats the water to 180° in the furnace, but by the time it gets to my bedroom on the second floor it is some degrees colder. As the heat disperses into the room the temperature is further reduced to room temperature, or 72°. Obviously, we would not expect the water to be hotter at any point in the pipes and radiators than in the furnace itself. By repeating a point in different ways, a speaker can emphasize without making the material monotonous.

We have observed the manner in which reinforcement, emphasis, and repetition enhance effective informative discourse. Repetition and emphasis are particularly crucial for effective informing, and reinforcement is essential when the information is conveyed in numerous sessions over a period of time.

Projects

1. After you have prepared an outline for a speech. re-examine it critically and decide which ideas need emphasis and reinforcement. Write in the margin of the outline what means you will use to achieve these ends.
2. Be prepared to discuss the means of emphasis and reinforcement employed by one of your professors in a lecture.
3. Write a paragraph about the emphasis and reinforcement employed in one of your classmate's speeches.

8.

INFORMATIVE COMMUNICATION

AND THE PERSON

This book has explored the multiple varieties of informative tasks in order to create a rhetoric of informing. Such a rhetoric, however, must be more than merely descriptive if it is to be responsible. The additional question must be raised as to what responsible informative communication's best or highest form is. The thesis of this chapter is that informative communication becomes degenerative whenever the integrity of the auditor is violated.

To see how depersonalization of the listener takes place, let us imagine that Professor Steven Stitzelbaum has been experimenting with submarines propelled electromagnetically. The city newspaper prints an account of his work and successes, which results in an invitation to speak to the Yacht Club. Dr. Stitzelbaum accepts the invitation and begins to prepare his speech. He decides that most members of the club will have little background for understanding the basic electromagnetic forces involved. Therefore he will give some of the history of the research and the results to date, but will ignore the theoretical problems involved because they are technical and difficult to explain to a lay audience. Some of the results of the experimentation are inconclusive, and various hypotheses have been advanced to explain the discrepancies. But Dr. Stitzelbaum has his own view which he decides to present without mentioning the others, thinking the additional views will only serve to confuse matters. So convinced is he of his conclusion that he even fails to indicate that other explanations have been offered. The speech is delivered and a question period follows. During the question period Sol Sauser asks Dr. Stitzelbaum to explain how an electromagnetic force can propel a submarine. Stitzelbaum replies that the explanation requires technical background and that time will not permit him to explain the theory involved.

In this example certain features of an approach to informative communication emerge. Since Dr. Stitzelbaum has little respect for the ability of his listeners to grasp what he has to say, he merely presents the results of the experiments without explaining how the results were obtained. He further indicates his lack of respect for the audience by presenting controversial explanations as if they were established and widely accepted. He knows that because of the audience's lack of knowledge, no one would be able to dispute his word anyway. Finally, he assumes that his approach is justified because the communication of technical materials to a lay audience is difficult and little can be done about it. The result is that the informative communication is degenerate because Stitzelbaum has assigned his auditors to an inferior status which he is unwilling to help them overcome.

In order to develop in greater depth the view that informative communication becomes degenerate when the person of the audience is disregarded, we need to (1) discuss what it means to be a person, (2) identify ways of depersonalizing informative communication, (3) locate a generative role for informative communication, and (4) identify a way of communicating so as to preserve the integrity of the person.

THE PERSON

A considerable body of current literature discusses the meaning of *person*. Other terms sometimes employed are *self, selfhood, ego,* and *transcendental ego.* The word person is used here because it has a public-language meaning which fits our purposes. Because our focus in this book is on communication, space does not permit a presentation of the various views of personhood. As used in this book, the word person means someone who asserts a view of the world in a system, a model, or a myth, and this world view provides a perspective from which to interpret facts. If a speaker takes up the burden of personhood by affirming a world view and holds this right inviolable, he must grant the same privilege to every other being who can assert, or—in other words—every other person. This means that what he communicates he is bound to communicate in such a way that the other person is protected and enhanced. In order to do this he needs to help the listener locate the assertions that are being made in the communication—that is, the system in which the facts are couched. If the speaker helps the auditor locate the assertions in this manner, as the auditor grows in understanding he will be able to make his own assertions, and hence become a "person" in the matter under consideration. It was this task which Dr. Stitzelbaum refused to undertake.

If the person is to be considered, the end of informative communication is not merely to set forth facts and conclusions so that they may be stored and reproduced. Computers now in operation have much greater capacity for information storage and retrieval than men, and computer capacity is rapidly increasing. With such machinery on the scene, it seems a waste of time merely to set facts before an audience. What the person can do, which computers as yet fail to accomplish, is to comprehend complex concepts and create new ones. The function of informative communication in our society should therefore be to present information so that presuppositions are disclosed. In this manner the assertive nature of information is manifest, and the persons of both the communicator and auditor are enhanced.

DEPERSONALIZED INFORMATIVE COMMUNICATION

The two main reasons why informative communication becomes depersonalized are, first, that speakers view those who are not sophisticated in the subject matter as subordinate persons and, second, that "true" knowledge is nonpersonal and hence the communication of it is depersonalized. Routine matters, of which there are many, demand depersonalized communication, but more and more such communication is being taken over by computers, thereby freeing man for more personal communication tasks. Our chief concern here is the communication of man with man in situations that make personal communication desirable.

Treating auditors as subordinate persons

Dr. Stitzelbaum was guilty of treating the members of the Yacht Club as subordinate persons, or really not as persons at all. He decided they could not understand the theory behind his experimentation, and he was unwilling to do anything to prepare them for such understanding. A speaker who makes this assumption says, in effect, that it is his privilege to know the theory of his subject area, and that of his audience to know only the facts and conclusions. He assumes that he himself is a person, whereas his auditors are inferior machine-like or slave-like organisms. One is, of course, limited in the knowledge of presuppositions he can communicate to audiences having certain age levels, experience, and intelligence levels. But if he is concerned with advancing his auditors' status as persons in a subject matter, he must give them more than mere facts and conclusions. In every available way, he helps them appreciate presuppositions (affirmations) and understand why they are advanced. In this manner he helps them to arrive at the stage where they are no longer novices, but can enter the discussion on an argumentative level with other specialists. This task of preparing for personhood is a very important one and hence the need to give attention to informative communication.

As we have emphasized, the refusal of a speaker to treat his auditors as persons is one reason why communication may degenerate. Dr. Stitzelbaum treats other specialists as persons, but all learners or lay persons as a subspecies of persons. In fact, some communicators or groups wish to build a pseudo-intellectual atmosphere in which it is understood that only the experts can comprehend the mysteries of their discipline. Their language betrays this desire. For example, "The reasons why space is curved are so complex that only physicists can understand it." The communicator who takes this attitude either wishes to maintain the isolation of his authoritativeness or is merely too lazy to search out means through which the audience can comprehend the subject. J. Bronowski has affirmed his conviction that the complexities of science *can* be conveyed.

> I believe that it is easy for a man who likes conversation and to read the second leader now and again to be comfortable with the large ideas of science; as easy as it is for a scientist to have a fancy for biography. The difficulties are those of language and the personal fear of what is unfamiliar. These are merely fed by those enthusiastic scientists who write as if the layman were to be pitied, and treat him as an erring would be scientist who ought to be converted to an interest in the nucleus.[1]

Presuppositionless information

Another major reason why some communicators fail to indicate the assertions involved in a subject is that they maintain that information can be so certain as to be free from presuppositions. If one points out that in many cases specialists disagree, this expert is likely to respond that schools of thought which oppose his are incorrect, and to bring them into the discussion is to court confusion. Others, however, present material as if it were presuppositionless because they are not knowledgeable enough to be aware of the presuppositions.

1. J. Bronowski, *The Common Sense of Science* (New York: Vintage Books, n.d.), p. 8.

Many claims have been made as to the universality and certainty of knowledge, but perhaps that made by logical positivism is the most developed and systematic. The more popular form of scientific positivism affirms that whenever a scientist establishes a conclusion empirically, the conclusion is certain and without presuppositions. Those who hold this view can readily distinguish between informative and persuasive discourse, since informative discourse concerns facts which have been established by science, and persuasion has to do with any matter which has not yet been thus established.

If the assumption of positivism is correct, science moves slowly, establishing as it goes propositions that are certain, ever traveling to new frontiers, building upon previously verified propositions. Scientific knowledge is therefore characterized by the absence of all personal belief. If this is the case, the person of the creator of knowledge and the person of the audience both become irrelevant in the communicative act. The positivist view, however, has been criticized in recent years.[2] The critics claim that significant knowledge is couched in a world view, system, or model and always contains a personal element — that is, an assertion on the part of the person interpreting the facts. Bronowski makes the point in discussing Newton's mechanics:

> What Newton did now was to suppose that the general rules which fair-sized masses seem to obey are true of every piece of matter, whatever its kind or its size. And having decided to try this thought, he made himself a new world of his own, which he built up from minute pieces of matter each following the same laws or axioms. This world is just as much a construction as the abstract world of geometry which Euclid built up out of his axioms.[3]

Bronowski goes on to show that the breakdown of the Newtonian world view was itself the emergence of a new "world" which was constructed from the assertion that the movement of particles of atoms is indeterminate, and hence must be conceived through the use of statistical models. Systems, philosophies, and models are all assertions about the world; and when the informative communicator accepts this he recognizes his information not as factual by some universal criterion, but as personal in nature.

2. Among the critics are: Karl Popper, *Conjectures and Refutations* (New York: Basic Books, 1962) and Michael Polanyi, *Personal Knowledge* (Chicago: University of Chicago Press, 1958).
3. J. Bronowski, *The Common Sense of Science*, pp. 35ff.

Acceptance of this view concerning the personal nature of truth does not result in a thoroughgoing relativism, since some specific propositions such as "the moon revolves about the earth," "wind sways trees," and "the sun rises earlier in the northern hemisphere in the summer than in the winter" are accepted as predictable with certainty. But as one moves to more significant propositions, such as, "the orbit of the moon is influenced by the gravitational forces in the solar system," "sunspots influence air currents on earth," and "the tilt of the earth determines the time of sunrise," he is starting to work with propositions involving presuppositions. When one reaches this point, an element of personal knowledge enters the picture; for this reason, a strong personal element must be recognized in the content of informative discourse. The Dr. Stitzelbaums of this world thus ignore the personal nature of information by presenting only their own views, and they deny to their auditors the right (which is the right of the person) to hear opposing views and make up their own minds, or at least to hold the matter in abeyance until they are capable of making up their own minds.

THE ROLE OF INFORMATIVE COMMUNICATION

The role of informative communication represents a generative function of preparing the uninitiated for emerging into "personhood" in a discipline. This is a very crucial task, hence the importance of informative communication. If one begins with the person, persuasion is the primary mode of human communication; but in order to persuade, one must have a grasp of background presuppositions and information; or, in other words, at some time or another one needs to have been informed. But when informative discourse becomes the only mode of communication, it has overstepped its bounds and becomes degenerate inasmuch as it has excluded the person.

Those who have already become knowledgeable in a field do not inform each other, but rather utilize persuasion or argument as their predominate form of communication. Even in science, the main type of discourse among specialists is argumentative, a fact which scientists and — perhaps more specifically — philosophers of science tend to forget when they frame statements about scientific knowledge. Communication dealing with the frontiers of science is always argumentative, and if, over the years, consensus is reached, it is only after considerable argument. The argument of these formulative stages is afterwards forgotten, but science advances only by re-examining positions which have become accepted. Informative communication serves to prepare for personhood; in this role information presented as impersonal is inadequate. To prepare an audience for personhood, the speaker must help presuppositions emerge so that, when properly understood, they can be argued.

PRESERVING THE INTEGRITY OF THE PERSON

It may be difficult for a communicator to present presuppositions so that they may be understood by an audience, especially if the audience has little background in the subject. Some communicators complain that to lay out presuppositions makes the materials so involved that it serves only to confuse the auditors. They therefore feel justified in presenting only their conclusions under the claim that an audience with inadequate background will be unable to comprehend more. Also, some listeners would rather be spared the struggle with difficult concepts, and thus accord more popularity to the speaker or lecturer who leaves presuppositions out. These difficulties cannot be denied, but the task is not hopeless.

To a degree, the chapter on clarification provided means by which a communicator may take into account the person of the audience. The best way a complex idea can be explained and the presuppositions brought into the open is by presenting the history of development or discovery. Through this avenue the personal element is brought out in two ways: first, by explaining the manner in which something is developed or discovered, the presuppositions of the time become clear and the thinking of the person making the new assertion emerges against this background. One is thus able to follow the mental struggle, and hence is better able to appreciate and comprehend the concepts which emerge from the struggle. The second way the history of development is helpful is that it either provides a movement from a simple to a more complex idea, or else it provides a sharp contrast with other ideas from the contemporary setting. Through these means the personal element of information is disclosed and the person of the audience is accommodated.

One can find much informative discourse based on a history of development. J. Bronowski, in *The Common Sense of Science*, discusses the change from the world of Newton to the world of modern statistical physics. Newton's system worked for the movement of large bodies on which he focused his interest; but when scientists came to deal with the particles of atoms, Newton's mechanical model no longer helped explain what was observed. It then became necessary to employ statistical models. From Bronowski's book one gets a clear conception as to why Newton saw the world as he did and why scientists today view it differently. Bronowski also presents alternate views such as that of Einstein. From reading Bronowski's book, one not only understands some of the facts of modern physics, but also realizes why the physicist thinks as he does. The personal element in physics thus becomes obvious.

Bertrand Russell in *A History of Western Philosophy* gives special attention to the climate out of which the philosophies emerged. In his introduction he states:

> My purpose is to exhibit philosophy as an integral part of social and political life; not as the isolated speculations of remarkable individuals, but as both an effect and a cause of the character of the various communities in which different systems flourished.[4]

E. C. Large in his book *The Advance of the Fungi* presents a detailed account of the manner in which the early theory of fungi emerged and the manner in which it was modified and became more complex as biologists hit upon new discoveries and adopted new presuppositions.[5] From this book emerges the thesis, argued here, that contemporary scientific views have been hammered out by humans, and contain at least remnants of the personal thinking of the people who framed and modified the views. It is therefore the responsibility of the communicator to treat the facts as personal interpretations.

Another effective vehicle for pointing out the personal nature of information is the analogy. This is especially true if the communicator discloses that the facts in a particular subject are interpreted in terms of a particular analogy or model. Previously we have pointed out that for Newton, the model was the machine because of its regularity. For the biologist, the beads on a string served as an analogy for genes until the spiral staircase was found to be a better analogy in some cases. For the contemporary biologist, DNA provides information about the life processes in the same manner that the computer card feeds information to the computer in order that it can carry out the appropriate calculations. In discussing the analogies and the reasons why they were selected, the communicator discloses the manner in which people conceive the world. By pointing out these features about the analogy, the personal element in information becomes obvious. At the same time the complex material is more readily understood, since the analogy is normally a comparison with something already experienced by the auditor.

The significant task of the informative speaker is to elevate the

4. Bertrand Russell, *A History of Western Philosophy* (New York: Simon and Schuster, Inc., 1959), p. 10.

5. E. C. Large, *Advance of the Fungi* (New York: Dover Publications, Inc., 1962).

listener to personhood. But once the task has been accomplished, communication moves on to argumentation and persuasion. The task is similar to that of an educational institution which eagerly prepares its scholars for the day of graduation so that they may go on to other accomplishments. The task of informative speaking is a significant one since it is concerned with preparing people for personhood. Thus, informing as a communication mode always works eagerly for its own demise so that the person of the auditor can emerge. It is hoped that this book has made a contribution by presenting a type of informative communication which leads to that vital end.

Projects

1. Write a short paper about the lecturing techniques of two or three professors, discussing whether or not you think they treat their students as persons. Indicate the clues on which you have based your judgment.
2. Do newscasters and news magazines treat their listeners and readers as persons? Why do you make this claim?
3. Read an essay in a scientific magazine intended for general consumption such as *Scientific American* or *Natural History*. Does the author attempt to help the reader understand the presuppositions upon which the explanation of his material is based?
4. What role do you think informative communication plays in the profession you expect to enter? Is it a generative, positive role?
5. Are you confronted with much depersonalized communication during the course of the day? Is it all a threat to you? What kind is and what kind is not? Offer examples.
6. If auditors show a lack of interest in the presuppositions upon which results are based, is a speaker justified in leaving out that part of the discussion and moving on? Explain your position.
7. Is it possible that a speaker may be unaware of the presuppositions in the information he is giving out? If so, is it because of lack of preparation on his part?

RECOMMENDED READINGS

Four main disciplines contribute to our understanding of informative communication and the recommended readings are divided accordingly.

Speech Books

ARNOLD, CARROLL C., DOUGLAS EHNINGER, and JOHN C. GERBER, *The Speaker's Resource Book* (Glenview, Ill.: Scott, Foresman and Company, 1966). This book contains a number of speeches which are primarily designed to inform. See the list under "Classification of the speeches according to purpose."

AUGUSTINE, *De Catechizandis Rudibus*. The first part instructs the priest in the teaching of the catechism. It is thus an early attempt to set forth a rhetoric of informing.

BACON, FRANCIS, *Advancement of Learning*. Of interest is Bacon's view of the type of communication important for the advancement of science.

BERLO, DAVID K., *The Process of Communication* (New York: Holt, Rinehart & Winston, Inc., 1960). The point of view is taken in this book that all communication is persuasive. It provides an important contrast with the point of view worked out here.

BORMANN, ERNEST G., *Theory and Research in the Communicative Arts* (New York: Holt, Rinehart & Winston, Inc., 1965). A significant working out of a rhetoric as informed by contemporary science.

BRYANT, DONALD C., and KARL R. WALLACE, *Fundamentals of Public Speaking* (New York: Appleton-Century-Crofts, 1960). The section on informative speaking in this book is the most extensively worked out of modern speech texts.

CAMPBELL, GEORGE, *The Philosophy of Rhetoric*, ed. Lloyd F. Bitzer (Carbondale, Ill.: Southern Illinois University Press, 1963). Campbell calls the attention of rhetoricians to the intent of the speaker. One of these intents is the enlightening of the understanding.

GILMAN, WILBUR E., BOWER ALY, and LOREN D. REID, *The Fundamentals of Speaking* (New York: The Macmillan Company, 1951). Contains a chapter on informative speaking which points in the direction of an audience-centered rhetoric of information.

Korzybski, Alfred, *Science and Sanity* (Lancaster, Pa.: Science Press, 1941). Korzybski's theory of communication would make all communication informative, but on a different ground than those proposed here.

McBurney, James H., and Ernest J. Wrage, *The Art of Good Speech* (New York: Prentice-Hall, Inc., 1953). A chapter on informative speaking is titled "The Methods of Reporting."

Ross, Raymond S., *Speech Communication Fundamentals and Practice* (Englewood Cliffs, N.J.: Prentice-Hall, Inc., 1965). A book which takes into account recent psychology, the insights from which show up to some extent in the chapter on informing.

Books on Communication

Cherry, Colin, *On Human Communication* (Cambridge, Mass.: The Technology Press, Massachusetts Institute of Technology, 1957). A significant work on communication from the standpoint of the message.

Bellow, Francis, *Readings in Communication from* Fortune, ed., Francis William Weeks (New York: Holt, Rinehart & Winston, Inc., 1961). Written in popular style for businessmen.

Hovland, Carl I., Irving L. Janis, and Harold H. Kelley, *Communication and Persuasion* (New Haven, Conn.: Yale University Press, 1953). This work is mostly on persuasion, but contains a few statements which support the point of view regarding informing presented here.

Miller, G. A., *Language and Communication* (New York: McGraw-Hill Book Company, 1951). An important early work on communication theory.

Psychology Books

Carroll, John B., *Language and Thought* (Englewood Cliffs, N.J.: Prentice-Hall, Inc., 1964). An introduction to a psychological view of language which commences with linguistics.

Ferster, C., and B. F. Skinner, *Schedules of Reinforcement* (New York: Appleton-Century-Crofts, 1957). Presents the Skinnerian approach to learning.

Hochberg, J. E., *Perception* (Englewood Cliffs, N.J.: Prentice-Hall, Inc., 1964). An introduction to perception which shows the possibility of ascertaining the meaning of feedback.

Kimble, G. A., *Hilgard and Marquis' Conditioning and Learning* (New York: Appleton-Century-Crofts, 1957).

Lambert, William W., and Wallace E. Lambert, *Social Psychology* (Englewood Cliffs, N.J.: Prentice-Hall, Inc., 1964). Chapter 3 provides insight into perceiving group attitudes.

Mednick, Sarnoff A., *Learning* (Englewood Cliffs, N.J.: Prentice-Hall, Inc., 1964). An introduction to learning which indicates the classical approaches and later modifications.

Stephenson, William, *The Study of Behavior* (Chicago: University of Chicago Press, 1953). Representative of the newer psychology which is more individual centered.

Philosophical Books

Alston, William P., *Philosophy of Language* (Englewood Cliffs, N.J.: Prentice-Hall, Inc., 1964). An introduction to language which objects to the referent theory.

Austin, J. L., *Philosophical Papers* (Oxford: Oxford University Press, 1961). Presents interesting revisions in the logical positivist view of language.

Bronowski, J., *The Common Sense of Science* (New York: Vintage Books, n.d.). Presents a view of science which sees scientific conclusions as more than merely factual.

Langer, Susanne K., *Philosophy in a New Key* (New York: Mentor Books, 1958). A discussion of language which recognizes different uses of language in different disciplines.

Popper, Karl, *Conjectures and Refutations* (New York: Basic Books, Inc., Publishers, 1962). Argues for a view of science in which argumentation is significant.

Richards, I. A., *The Philosophy of Rhetoric* (New York: Oxford University Press, Inc., 1936). A discussion of language in which its analogical nature is recognized.

Ullmann, S., *Semantics: An Introduction to the Science of Meaning* (New York: Barnes & Noble, Inc., 1962). Representative of philosophical approaches to semantics.

Wittgenstein, Ludwig, *Philosophical Investigations* (New York: The Macmillan Company, 1963). An important book by the father of British language analysis.

INDEX

Allport, Gordon W., 25
Alston, William P., 59–60
Aly, Bower, 20
Analogies, 80–85
Aquinas, Thomas, 65, 68, 91
Aristotle, 2, 16, 25, 65
Arnold, Carroll C., 90
Atonement, 64
Audience, attitude toward topic, 26; factor analysis of, 28–32; history of nature of, 25–26; interest, 36; nature of, 24; oriented structures, 44ff.; receptiveness to communication, 9–10, 21–22
Augustine, 2, 7, 9
Aulèn, Gustaf, 64
Aural aids, 90
Austin, J. L., 76

Bacon, Francis, 7, 72, 86
Bellows, Francis, 84
Berlo, David, 15
Bernstein, Leonard, 90
Black, Edwin, 2
Bormann, Ernest G., 8
Branching technique, 40, 49–52
Bronowski, J., 8, 62, 106–107, 109
Bryant, Donald C., 17, 39

Campbell, George, 2, 9, 17
Carroll, J. B., 63
Cassirer, Ernst, 72–73
Cherry, Colin, 18
Cicero, 2
Clarification—forms of, analogy, 80–85 (figurative, 80; literal, 80; literary, 80); contrast, 84–85; example, 75–79; history of development, 86–89; statistics, 78–79; visual and aural aids, 89–96
Classifying speeches, by audience, 19; by message, 18; by situation, 16; by speaker intent, 17
Cohen, Morris, 82
Communication models, 95
Computers, 31, 35–36
Contrast, 84–85

Dalton, John, 87
Depersonalized informative communication, 105
Descartes, 7–8, 59, 88
Dialectical materialism, 90
Dream theory, 29–30, 32–33, 87–88

Ear, the human, 92–95
Education, 4, 11
Ehninger, Douglas, 90
Ehrensberger, Raymond, 100
Emotion, 15
Emphasis, 99–101
Examples, 75–79
Existentialism, 62, 77–78, 85, 90

Faulkner, William, 73–74
Federal Reserve System, 91–92
Ferster, C., 98
Flesch, Rudolph, 70
Flow charts, 46–47
Freud, Sigmund, 29, 32–33, 87–88

General Semantics, 18, 60, 85
Genetics, 74–75
Gerber, John, 90
Gilman, Wilbur E., 20
Glassmaking, 5
Goldwater, Barry, 17
Guilds, 3

Hebrew poetry, 67
Heidegger, Martin, 62
Hilgard, Ernest R., 39, 98
History of Development, 86–89
Hochberg, J. E., 28
Hovland, Carl I., 20
Hume, David, 8, 42
Husserl, Edmund, 69

Information theory, 18
Informative speaking, conditions for, 6, 10–12; history of, 1–12 (ancient, 1–6; modern, 6–10;